the way of
HOPE

the way of

HOPE

A Fresh Perspective on Sexual Identity,
Same-Sex Marriage, and the Church

MELISSA FISHER

BakerBooks

a division of Baker Publishing Group
Grand Rapids, Michigan

Published by Baker Books
a division of Baker Publishing Group
P.O. Box 6287, Grand Rapids, MI 49516-6287
www.bakerbooks.com

Printed in the United States of America

Library of Congress Cataloging-in-Publication Data is on file at the Library of Congress, Washington, DC.

ISBN 978-0-8010-7295-6

Some names and details have been changed to protect the privacy of the individuals who have shared their stories with the author.

17 18 19 20 21 22 23   7 6 5 4 3 2 1

To Kayla,
I am forever grateful God let me be your little sister.
Thank you for always protecting and loving me
no matter what path I traveled on.
I love you.

Contents

Foreword

Life is often filled with unexpected journeys.

When I felt called to start a church in Austin, God started me on one such journey. I sensed him asking me to "create a place where all people—including the gay community—can seek me and find me." I said, "Okay, but you have to show me how 'cause I don't have a clue."

As I obediently followed his invitation to create a church where broken, hurt, dechurched, and unchurched people could explore and find faith, God began to grow my heart, compassion, and understanding for those searching for answers to their faith questions, including people in the LGBT community. I've had the opportunity to get to know many amazing men and women of various sexual identities and backgrounds and to be a part of their journey, learn about their lives, and hear their complex stories. Most of all, I've had the privilege of getting to watch as they found a love that surpassed all others. That love walked each of them down unique paths of understanding, growth, and freedom.

Eight years ago, I got to know Melissa as she bravely pushed through the fears of judgment and rejection that many people face when pursuing faith and began attending Gateway. Since then, I've had the privilege of watching her grow and pursue spiritual maturity. She is now able to help others walk this path leading to greater life, love, and freedom. Melissa is one of the godliest women I know, and her life demonstrates the life and freedom Jesus purchased for all human beings.

In this book, Melissa takes you into her journey—a journey common to all people, gay or straight, searching for faith and navigating the confusing waters of the church and culture. On the one hand, there are churches that too easily shame and guilt people into external conformity, which creates religious Pharisees who look one way on the outside but who are rotting spiritually on the inside. On the other hand, there are churches that bend Scripture's teachings and make accommodations for those in all seasons and situations of life, which end up offering nothing different from the world and culture around them. This leaves people, including those scattered across the sexual identity map, trapped in hurt and pain; they long for the life God offers yet feel hopeless to find it. Neither way is what Jesus came to offer.

Melissa invites all, gay or straight, confused or secure in their identity, to consider another way—*the way of hope*. It's not a cookie-cutter, five-step way to go from being gay to straight. It's not a coercive way to make people change or to produce behavior modification. It's a personal way—uniquely crafted by the God who created each one of us—that offers life and freedom, joy and peace. It's a way that can't be controlled or put in a nice, neat box to be marketed in a church program. It's a way offered by a personal God to all . . . if you are willing.

If you're in the same-sex lifestyle and have found this book, my prayer is that you'll read it with curiosity and openness. Give yourself permission to let go of trying to figure out your sexual attraction or relationships; instead, be open to just looking intently at Jesus to see if he is as crazy in love with you as he is with Melissa. If so, seek him with all your heart, breathe, and do not fear. Jesus wants to give you something far better than you can imagine. Be brave, take the first step, and read this book.

If you are a family member or friend of someone in the gay lifestyle or a church leader or pastor, my prayer as you read is that you will listen, learn, and be open to considering a new way of relating to those with different sexual orientations, identities, and beliefs. I pray you will be inspired to get to know someone's story, usually of great pain, and be willing to walk alongside them and demonstrate how much they are worth to God. I pray this book leads you to move forward, able to show the love, compassion, and hope of Jesus because, thankfully, his love has the power to change us all.

John Burke
pastor of Gateway Church Austin,
author of *No Perfect People Allowed*
and *Imagine Heaven*

Introduction

The Road Not Taken

Two roads diverged in a yellow wood,
And sorry I could not travel both
And be one traveler, long I stood
And looked down one as far as I could
To where it bent in the undergrowth;

Then took the other, as just as fair,
And having perhaps the better claim,
Because it was grassy and wanted wear;
Though as for that the passing there
Had worn them really about the same,

And both that morning equally lay
In leaves no step had trodden black.
Oh, I kept the first for another day!
Yet knowing how way leads on to way,
I doubted if I should ever come back.

I shall be telling this with a sigh
Somewhere ages and ages hence:

> Two roads diverged in a wood, and I—
> I took the one less traveled by,
> And that has made all the difference.
>
> Robert Frost (1874–1963)[1]

Have you ever struggled with knowing which way to go? Been in one of those moments when you could go right or left and didn't know which way to choose? Stood staring at that fork in the road, wishing it was a knife or a spoon? Felt split in two by a split in the trail?

Which trail did you choose? Did you peer as far as the eye could see down both roads? Did you flip a coin, letting Lady Luck have her way? Or did you passively step aside and let someone else choose for you? What was the outcome?

As a former backpacking guide in Colorado, I have journeyed many a trail. Through the beautiful Rocky Mountains, I have hiked day and night in pursuit of the next summit, that next breath-taking view.

Many different trails or routes can take you up a mountain, and there are many different ways to hike or climb back down. As any hiker will tell you, the joy comes in the journey and in the beauty upon reaching your destination. But life on the trail can be hard. The weather can change unexpectedly. The air becomes thin. Sudden complications arise. And sometimes the beauty is difficult to see, as each step brings pain.

The trail you thought would bring joy brings pain. It's difficult to trudge on. You might wonder, what if? What if I had hiked faster? What if I had drunk less? What if I'd packed that extra protein bar? What if I had chosen someone else to travel with? What if I'd taken a different path or chosen a different trail?

We travel down countless trails in life—you've hiked yours, I've traveled mine—all in pursuit of that moment we're willing to bleed for, hoping it will be the moment when you finally feel alive. We hike and hike to reach that summit of security that promises freedom from the haunting insecurities only to see it for the false summit it is.

Have you heard of a *false summit*? Wikipedia defines it as "a peak that appears to be the pinnacle of the mountain, but upon reaching, it turns out the summit is higher. False peaks can have significant effects on a climber's psychological state by inducing feelings of dashed hopes or even failure."[2] It looks like the top, but its deception takes you emotionally lower than you were before. To put it bluntly, false summits, when hiking a long journey, suck.

You strain and bear the pain and finally reach the spot you've been working to obtain all day . . . all year . . . or all of your life only to be deflated by the higher peak staring down at you, taunting, laughing. The false summit leaves you broken, depressed, and struggling against the badge of failure you now wear.

My life has been full of false summits, hard trails, wrong turns. Has your life been filled with these too—trails that failed to bring you the joy you thought they would?

Glance back for a second. Why did you choose those trails? Did someone encourage you to go that way? Did the first steps seem to glimmer with excitement as they beckoned you their way or to offer some pot of gold at the end of the rainbow?

As a chord of Aerosmith's hit "Walk This Way" runs through my head, I wonder, did you? Did you walk the way you were told to by the voice in your head that was so convincing when it said, "This is *the way*! Travel this trail and you can have it *all*. Walk this way and you can have exactly what you have been looking for"? What did the voice promise you as you headed down the trail?

How's that trail working for you? From one traveler to another, is it time for a new trail?

This book is a collection of stories, wisdom, and views from some of the trails I've traveled down—some hard, many disappointing.

A few walked me into hell. Thankfully, as Frost eloquently stated, "way leads on to way," and all the other trails I've traveled have led to the one I'm now on.

Whatever trails you've been traveling down, I'd like to invite you to travel with me down a new one, *The Way of Hope*.

1

The Way of Perfection

They say that nobody is perfect. Then they tell you practice makes perfect. I wish they'd make up their minds.

Winston Churchill[1]

The roots of our pretend self lie in our childhood discovery that we can secure love by presenting ourselves in the most flattering light.

David Benner[2]

I used to want to be a boy.

Seriously, literally, have the surgery. Change the name. Live from the new identity. Be a boy, not a girl. That's what I wanted.

It seemed to make sense with how I felt on the inside. At that point in my life, my feelings had been all over the map. After all, I grew up in the church, left the church, dated boys, then left the guy scene and ended up in the same-sex lifestyle and a same-sex marriage. Somewhere, in the midst of all of that, I contemplated becoming a boy.

I want to get that out in the open and allow you the opportunity to digest it and decide if you want to keep reading. No hard feelings if you don't, but it might be like driving by a car wreck on the side of the road: you don't want to look but can't keep yourself from it. This story is a little like that.

I did want to be a boy. With everything in me, that's what I wanted—did, wanted, past tense.

Now, well, things are different. I'm no longer in the same-sex lifestyle, and I am very content and happy being a girl, a woman.

Not only did I return to church, but I'm also now actually on staff at a church. As part of my job, I help women learn how to be godly women. I know—big change. I mean, seriously, the girl who used to want to be a boy now leading women on how to be women? I shake my head in disbelief too as I reread it.

How does that happen? How did the men's cargo shorts, visor, and T-shirt–wearing girl become a skirt-and-don't-forget-the-accessories-loving woman?

"Way leads on to way."[3]

Let's start at the beginning—*The Way of Perfection*.

The Beginning

I am a born and raised Texas girl. I've owned a horse, cowboy boots, and a real cowboy belt with my name on it. I grew up in a conservative Christian home in central Texas, and as far back as I can remember, I was at church whenever the doors were open, which happened week in and week out, fifty-two weeks of the year. Every Sunday morning, Sunday night, and Wednesday night we were there (we being my older sister, my mom, and me). My father was there sometimes and even led singing in our a cappella, don't-believe-in-instruments-style service. At least I think he led singing. I have a vague memory of him being up front occasionally. Maybe he was reading Scripture or praying. I'm not sure, but I know he came sometimes when he wasn't traveling for work, and he traveled a lot. That I do remember . . . because of my Easy-Bake Oven.

Yes, I had an Easy-Bake Oven. Have you ever had one? It's a small, kid-sized, plastic oven that cooks little foods with a light-bulb, or at least it did then. As the independent baby of the family, I loved it because I could bake a cake all by myself. And I did. I'd take out that Pop-Tart-sized cake mix and add two or three spoonfuls of water with the purple spoon provided. Stir. Pour it in the tiny pan and voilà! One small, not-too-great-tasting cake! It was a big deal. I was making it one day for my dad, who was supposed to return home soon from traveling for work. I loved my dad, a lot. I thought he hung the moon or some other cliché phrase like that.

I made him that Easy-Bake chocolate cake with something resembling chocolate icing semi-smeared all over the top. Semi-smeared, because if you knew me well, you would know I am my mother's daughter and more chocolate icing would have gone into my mouth than on the cake. Chocolate icing, or anything chocolate for that matter, is one of my favorite food groups, along with popcorn, bacon, and pizza. Oh, and coffee. Praise God for coffee! In fact, I am drinking a nice cup right now. I'm trying to drink more green tea, but it's not working well. Coffee is like a warm, soothing mug of Jesus in my hand, and green tea . . . well . . . it isn't a mug of much. A mug of Jesus-blessed coffee is much better, because I like Jesus, a lot. Speaking of Jesus, I was talking about church, wasn't I? Not about baking or favorite food groups. Sorry. Like the funny dog in the movie *Up*, sometimes I chase squirrels.

So . . . let's get back to church.

Behave

For me, attending church brought mixed emotions. I hated having to get dressed up. In the early years, my mom would make me wear dresses, which felt like torture or child endangerment or some other call-CPS-worthy title. After all, I was a tomboy who liked to be outside exploring, playing soccer, or doing anything that wearing a dress would interfere with. I had the boots and the cowboy belt, remember? Looking pretty and wearing dresses were very important to my mom. Wearing a yellow ruffled dress or something similar, my sister and I would get loaded up into the car and head to church, where I would sit next to my mom and sing.

I loved to sing.

Did I mention we didn't have instruments in our church? That always made singing interesting, because there was nothing to drown out the fourteen off-pitch voices loudly singing "Rock of Ages" or "When the Roll Is Called Up Yonder" or some other old hymn. Don't get me wrong here. I am not in any way making fun of the hymns or the way in which they were sung. Hymns are still my favorites and can bring me to tears faster than any Chris Tomlin or Jesus Culture modern worship song can.

The point is that the churches I grew up in were smaller, more intimate. People knew instantly who coughed, sneezed, or fidgeted in the pew, and fidgeting wasn't allowed. This might be why I enjoyed the singing, because I got to stand up for at least one to three songs, depending on who was leading. Mostly, I loved singing because my mother sat next to me, and I loved to hear her sing. She had, in my opinion, the most beautiful voice, and I wanted to be able to sing just like her when I grew up.

I'd look pretty and sing pretty every Sunday morning. I'd do my best not to fidget, as it appeared to me at the time that God would be very disappointed in me if I moved too much or bothered my sister or breathed too loudly or needed to go to the bathroom during church. That was a no-no as well. For any of those behaviors I'd get a look, a talking-to, my hand slapped, or that extended hand-holding that wasn't really an "I'm holding your hand because I love you" message but more an "I am sending you a firm and controlled message to stop whatever nonsensical thing you are doing or you will be sorry" type of communication.

I'd try hard to be good, silent, and still like a statue (or a corpse) because movement of any kind was strongly discouraged. Drawing on paper or coloring during a service was strictly forbidden. Don't even think about doing that. I remember the first time I attended another church and saw a child drawing on paper during the service. I was so scared for him that God was going to be mad at him for not paying attention. I had learned well enough by then that you don't want to make God mad. I'd heard some of the stories from the Old Testament and knew God had a temper.

I'd listen, pay attention, and learn important things about God and about what the Bible said.

Pretty

Like the first Scripture I learned as a child: "Pretty is as pretty does." Do you know this verse? This passage comes from the book of First Opinions, chapter 4, verse 2, and was quoted regularly by my grandmother on my mom's side, whom we called Memaw. For those not familiar with the Bible, this saying isn't in it, and there isn't really a book of the Bible called First Opinions. Sometimes well-meaning folks preach morality statements more than actual Scripture, so it's hard to know the difference. Like a good dose of "Cleanliness is next to godliness." Or, "God helps those who help themselves." And, always popular during hard times, the friendly reminder "This too shall pass."

Growing up as an adventurous girl, I would regularly hear pretty is as pretty does preached to me anytime I did something less than ladylike or anything my grandmother didn't approve of. So, as a little girl who didn't like dresses or things of that nature, I heard it a lot. It felt like one of those sayings that people bought printed on stationery or coffee mugs or quilted on pillows they put on their fancy couches that no one ever sat on. My grandmother had one such couch in the front room. It was the stuffiest room in the house, and no one ever sat in there. The couch and chair were horribly firm and uncomfortable. Everything in there was breakable and not allowed to be touched. It would have been a perfect place for a crocheted "Pretty is as pretty does" pillow to reside.

The regularly preached passage embedded in me at an early age was "If you do pretty things, you will be pretty." Of course, any time I heard it, it was because I wasn't doing pretty. This led me down one path of thought: do good and I was good, do pretty and I was pretty.

The problem? I wasn't that good at being good, or so I thought. I didn't do things good enough or pretty enough. So naturally, I didn't feel pretty.

In fact, one of the first memories of a feeling I had about myself was anything but beautiful or delightful. It happened while sitting in the living room of my grandparents' house watching TV. The living room was a stark contrast to the front room, as you were allowed to move, breathe, and touch things. My grandfather had a plastic red-and-white fish that sat on the mantel above the fireplace, and when you opened its mouth, you found a smaller fish inside attached to a drawstring, which you could pull out and watch the big fish gobble back up. I am not sure why as a child watching the big red fish devour the little blue fish time and time again was so entertaining, but it was.

Maybe it was because my grandfather loved fishing and would take us all the time. I loved fishing with him and eating Chips Ahoy! cookies, which he kept in a yellow metal tin on his boat. The sun would warm the metal tin, causing the chocolate chips in the cookies to melt just a little, making them the best tasting Chips Ahoy! cookies I had ever eaten. His ring finger had been cut off just above his middle knuckle in a boating accident, and when I was a young child, my fingers perfectly curled around his nub, which I would hold on to as I walked beside him. He loved to play SKIP-BO and dominoes and every now and then would get so tickled playing that he would laugh so hard he would cry. Those were my favorite moments because my giant, gentle grandfather would express emotions otherwise hidden in his quiet, reserved nature. He was the perfect match for my grandmother, who always shared what she was thinking. Not that she was a Chatty Cathy. Oh no. My grandmother had a reserved way about her as well, but of the two, she was definitely the talker.

While sitting in the living room one evening, she shared what she was thinking so very politely. I was sitting on the floor in front of my grandmother, halfway between the television and the couch. This was the prime spot to sit in when you were the "remote control."

For you young'uns reading this, you may not be aware that at one time, the only way to change a channel on a TV was for some poor soul to have to get up off the couch or recliner, walk the entire distance across the living room, and turn the knob or push the button on the big, dresser-sized monstrosity of a TV.

Someone had to change the channel, and being the youngest of the family, I was naturally assigned the title of human remote control. I'd begrudgingly get up and turn the knob when *Happy Days* was over so the family could watch *The Dukes of Hazzard*, *M*A*S*H*, or some other epic early '80s show. *Three's Company*, *Mork and Mindy*, and *The Love Boat* were also worth crossing the expanse between the couch and the TV. But never would one turn the knob to watch shows like *Dynasty*, *Knots Landing*, or *Moonlighting*, as those were inappropriate with their sultry plots and scantily clothed actresses. And never, ever did we watch *Cheers*. It was a show filmed in a bar, and even as a young girl I knew that those people were bad, because drinking was bad, and watching that show might make me want to go to a bar and drink someday, and God wouldn't like that.

Because pretty is as pretty does. I must do pretty. I must do what's right all the time.

On that one day, sitting there in front of my grandmother watching TV, waiting to turn the channel, I did it: the sin of all sins. I picked my nose.

Yes, my prim and proper grandmother saw her granddaughter pick her nose. With the utmost gentleness, she cleared her throat and very properly said, "Melissa. . . . Do you need a Kleenex?"

I punctuate carefully here, as there was a distinct period and pause at the end of my name when she said it. There was no condemnation in her voice, no tone that something was wrong, evil, or out of line. But the clarity, pace, and posture in the way she said it made me feel something for the first time in my life: *shame*. I felt shame for what I had done. I had done bad, which meant only one thing. I was bad.

On that day, the first seed of shame quietly dropped into the soil of my heart, and the silent tears that fell inside my soul watered it, and the seed took root. Shame is that way. One simple moment in time, and the seed drops in.

When was it for you, the moment you first experienced shame? When did its roots begin to choke the life out of you? Shame is like that. It's the weed in your garden that seems impossible to kill.

Flawed

Shame and vulnerability researcher Dr. Brené Brown defines *shame* as "the intensely painful feeling or experience of believing we are flawed and therefore unworthy of acceptance and belonging."[4] In that moment, sitting on the tan carpet in the wood-paneled living room in my grandparents' house, I felt flawed, unworthy, alone. I felt *shame*.

Let's pause here to clarify that the seed of shame dropping into your soul is different from guilt growing in your garden. Guilt is the awareness or feeling that "I did something bad." Shame will turn that guilt from "I *did* bad" to "I *am* bad." That's what I felt in that moment. I was bad.

Today, I wonder, how could my grandmother have handled that moment differently? What could she have said or how could she have said it that would have enabled me to learn but not experience shame? I ask because shame is so enslaving. It is so painful. I wonder how many times I have said something similar to my nephews, friends, other adults, or kids I have taught. Have I ever dropped a seed of shame unknowingly into someone else's heart? I ask because only now, as an adult, am I even capable of beginning to understand what effect shame has had on me or how many times I've experienced it.

Like an unwelcome guest at a party, shame makes an appearance, and I have one immediate reaction: I want to hide. It's an interesting moment to pause and ponder. Hasn't shame always initiated hiding?

One Choice

Follow me on a journey back in time to a perfect garden—*the* garden, Eden—where Adam and Eve, the first people whom God created, enjoyed blissful freedom and beauty. They lived and walked and talked with God. There was only one rule. That big tree in the center? See its fruit? Don't pick it. Like picking your nose, it was an unacceptable thing to do times a million.

One rule, one tree, one fruit not to eat. Step with me into the story.

> Now the serpent was more crafty than any other beast of the field that the LORD God had made. He said to the woman, "Did God actually say, 'You shall not eat of any tree in the garden'?" And the woman said to the serpent, "We may eat of the fruit of the trees in the garden, but God said, 'You shall not eat of the fruit of the tree that is in the midst of the garden, neither shall you touch it, lest you die.'" But the serpent said to the woman, "You will not surely die. For God knows that when you eat of it your eyes will be opened, and you will be like God, knowing good and evil." (Gen. 3:1–5)

The snake tempted her with a little truth mixed with a little deception, and Eve had a choice. She looked at the fruit. She replayed and added to God's words. She thought. She judged. She rationalized. She saw profit for herself. She took it. She ate. Adam ate.

Instantly, everything changed. One choice, one moment, and shame entered in: "Then the eyes of both were opened, and they knew that they were naked. And they sewed fig leaves together and made themselves loincloths" (Gen. 3:7).

Did you see it—the moment of shame? "They knew that they were naked." Exposed, vulnerable, naked, and in need. Isn't that what shame does? It leads us to cover ourselves to keep people from seeing our nakedness, who we really are. Like Adam and Eve, we create and cover to protect ourselves. Then we hide.

An Inconvenient Habit

This next confession of shame is a little more embarrassing, but it might paint a clearer picture: I used to wet the bed.

While my exact age is unclear, the memories aren't. My mother, out of love, tried to help me learn to stop this awful and very inconvenient habit and purchased a bed-wetting pad with an alarm. It was a metal-looking pad placed under the sheet that had a sensor in it. When pottied upon, it would emit a loud alarm. The goal of such a device was to wake children up and alert them, so they could get up and go to the bathroom. Unfortunately for me, this 1980 system included an antiquated alarm that emitted this awfully loud NEE-eu NEE-eu, NEE-eu NEE-eu that scared me to death. I woke up lying in a wet pool with the sound of a French police car driving through my bedroom. It was loud enough to wake everyone in the house, and my mother would then come to my bedroom and change my sheets as I stood by, silently swallowing the shame I felt as, once again, I couldn't make it through the night.

Tragic and scarring, I know. She meant well. (It may have worked though. I haven't had a bed-wetting problem since.) The point of the confession? It was another deposit in my bank of shame.

A Liar

Looking back, I recall one more deposit that occurred at an early age.

I was riding in the car with my mom on the way to day care. She very kindly asked if I had bubble gum in my pocket. I politely replied, "No ma'am," as gum was not allowed at school. Unfortunately, my little devious brain had not calculated that the two pieces of three-cent Super Bubble bubble gum I had stuffed in my little pocket looked more like protruding mountains than the invisible pieces of yumminess I thought I was hiding. My mother dug her fingers into my pocket, fished out the sugary blessings, and said the nine most horrific words a child could ever hear: "We will deal with this when you get home!"

With tears streaming down my face, I was dropped off to face the eight-hour day of mental torture ahead of me. What happened later that day has stuck with me forever. While I didn't face the guillotine, I did get the belt, which, in the late '70s and early '80s, was allowed and encouraged, at least in my conservative, Bible-belt-wearing family.

Everyone I knew got spanked, and anyone older than you by twelve years or more could spank you. Your rear was free game at that time if you were a kid. It's just the way things were. I know that for some, spankings were more abusive in nature and done out of anger, rage, or hate instead of love. I didn't experience that, but this isn't about the pros and cons of spanking. It's about the extremely odd, rare, and honestly unexplainable moment that happened *after* a particular spanking.

My mother picked me up from the bedroom (where I had been spanked) and carried me into the kitchen, which she had *never* done before. She walked to the oven, which had been preheated, opened the door, and leaned me over so I could feel the heat. She then asked, "Melissa, do you feel how hot that is?"

With tears streaming, I replied in a scared, shaky voice, "Yu-yu-yeeesss maa-ma'am."

She said, "Well, that's nothing compared to how hot it is in hell, and that's where you'll go if you keep lying."

I've never lied since.

At least I wish I could say that. But I can't, because I have . . . more times than I'd like to admit.

That moment didn't teach me not to lie. I wish it had. I know my mother meant well in trying to teach me to be good. While this technique is creative in nature, I highly recommend never using it in your own parenting. It won't keep your kid from lying. What it did do was throw gasoline on the fire of shame and fear that had begun to ignite in me.

The Rules

Pretty is as pretty does, right? Like Adam and Eve, I began to know what I had to do when I didn't do pretty. I knew I needed to cover. I knew I needed to hide. The fig leaf I decided I could best hide behind was . . . perfection.

Whatever you do, do it right! After all, God is always watching.

> Make the list.
> Check it twice.
> Keep all the rules.
> He'll think you're nice.

Off with my little poem in my head I went. With the winds of shame pushing at my back, I stepped forward and began my journey down the path of perfection. A baby legalist was born.

Do you know the term *legalism*? Like all isms, it's not something you want to strive for or have as a character trait. Legalism is defined as a "strict, often too strict, and literal adherence to law."[5] Follow the law. Follow the rules.

I liked rules. You could hide behind them quite nicely. The simple rule about rules: keep them and all will be nice.

For those of you familiar with the Bible, you'll understand this one: I loved the Law.

For those of you who don't crack open the Bible too often, in Old Testament times God had a guy named Moses write down a bunch of rules for how the Israelites were to live. A big list of things they were to do or not do. The religious leaders who were really good at following them in the New Testament were known as Pharisees.

As a little girl, I started storing rules in my head. They weren't as detailed or as complex as the laws the Israelites had, but then again, I was only six-ish at the time. They were being spoken and/or properly modeled at all times, which was a problem, because Jesus came so that we didn't have to worry about keeping rules or laws. (We weren't very good at keeping them anyway.) As a little girl, I never got that memo. Instead, my parents, grandparents, teachers, church, and so on all sent messages to me on how to live "right" or do "right." Through my "pretty is as pretty does" filter, I took those messages and turned them into rules I had to keep so that I could be "right."

I became the good kid, the rule follower, the peacekeeper.

Praise

Yes, I became a professional observer of the world around me. I would watch and learn for the new rules I needed to live by. Following the rules brought peace and attention, and my addictive personality would soon learn that if you not only followed the rules but also excelled at them, you would get something even better than attention. You would get praise!

Receiving praise from others became my drug of choice. Throughout my life, the voice in my head would haunt me and whisper, "Do it right and they will praise you." Yes, just one more puff on the pipe of pleasure from the praise of people. It would be impossible to make it through the day without this drug in my system, and the voice only got louder as I grew older. Other lies would soon follow: "If they don't praise you, they don't like you. If they don't like you, they will leave you." The only balm that seemed to soothe the wound of abandonment that took over my life, like a terminal cancer, was the pleasure I could earn from people. So I began hustling for approval.

Yes, I even started hustling God, earning favor, working hard to earn his praise.

So began my journey of saving myself, checking one box at a time like a good little Pharisee.

☑ Don't talk back.
☑ Be still in church.
☑ Don't run in the store.
☑ Use a tissue.
☑ Don't smack your gum.
☑ Don't fight with your sister.
☑ Don't cuss.
☑ Make good grades.
☑ Don't dance.
☑ Don't drink.
☑ Don't have sex with boys.
☑ Don't embarrass the family.
☑ Make Mom happy.
☑ Be the best.

Check.
Check.
Check.

Make the list.
Check it twice.

Keep all the rules.
He'll think you're nice.
Earn.
Perform.
Repeat.
Earn.
Perform.
Repeat.
A good little Pharisee you will be.

Perfection

The Pharisees, religious leaders, were known for and prided themselves on keeping every law perfectly. They were so good, in fact, that they often had the entire Torah (the first five books of the Bible) memorized perfectly. They pretended to be all about God, but when Jesus came in the flesh, they wanted nothing to do with him except to kill him—and they did.

Why such hatred? Because Jesus saw through them. He saw past their rule keeping and legalistic living to their prideful, self-righteous hearts beneath. They didn't want him to be God, because they enjoyed being their own gods.

If you're new to Jesus, there is one thing you will learn as you get to know him: he is not a big fan of prideful people, especially arrogant religious leaders who constantly turn down their noses at others. In fact, he had so much against the Pharisees that he gave them seven warnings, accusations, or woes (depending on the Bible translation you use) about things they were doing wrong. He was so passionate about their prideful living that he called them hypocrites, blind guides, and snakes or a "brood of vipers" (Matt. 23:33). Strong language, I know!

Listen in to Jesus as he warns them:

> Woe to you, scribes and Pharisees, hypocrites! For you clean the
> outside of the cup and the plate, but inside they are full of greed and

self-indulgence. You blind Pharisee! First clean the inside of the cup and the plate, that the outside also may be clean. (Matt. 23:25–26)

How kind of Jesus to put this type of living into clear perspective. A life of prideful perfectionism is not the way to go. Focusing on outward behavior will never bring you life. But before we start judging the Pharisees too harshly for being so externally focused, I need to pause and remind myself and you that I was one. I wanted everyone to look at my outward deeds so they wouldn't see what I was inwardly.

Perfectionism is "a self-destructive and addictive belief system that fuels this primary thought: 'If I look perfect, live perfectly, and do everything perfectly, I can avoid or minimize the painful feelings of shame, judgment, and blame.'"[6] In those early moments as a little girl, I didn't want to ever feel those feelings of shame again.

Decades later I found myself, like the Pharisees, wrapped in a web of addiction and an absolute love of not only getting it right but also being the *best*. I wore perfectionism as a badge of honor for all to see while I hummed along:

> Look at my badge.
> Isn't it neat?
> If you could be better,
> You could be like me.

It's Okay, I Can Manage

It's as if my life was a vending machine and the same coin was dropped in day after day, week after week, year after year. One side of the coin was labeled *Pride* and the other side *Fear*. Whichever side faced up as you slid it into the machine didn't matter, as the same perfection-filled performance was dispensed out in my life. I couldn't stop, and honestly, I didn't want to. My pride was addicted to my perfectionism, and my fear couldn't handle showing up any other way.

I'd make the list, check it twice. You've been reading enough to know by now that I'd do anything to get everything right. This would be one of the largest stumbling blocks I'd trip over time and time again in my life. The real problem with my perfectionism was that I was constantly looking at *me*. I was looking at my performance, looking for more praise.

Perfectionism puts you on a path of self-sufficiency that makes everything, including salvation, about you. What I would later learn was that my own self-righteousness was the wall standing in the way of experiencing the fullness of what God had for me—grace. As Edward Welch so perfectly states, "And if we think we are usually good, then God is usually irrelevant."[7]

Ouch. If I am honest, God was irrelevant. Self-made saviors don't need someone else to save them. My perfectionism made God present but irrelevant. This would cause me many years later to wreck the train that my life was traveling on. As I stared down the tracks looking at the rubble, I realized they were leading nowhere. Like a small electric train circling under the Christmas tree, the way of perfectionism kept me circling round and round, going nowhere.

Yes, the train of perfection fell off its tracks, and I couldn't do anything about it. But that's a couple of chapters away.

For now, we have a nose-picking, bed-wetting little girl full of shame becoming a perfectionistic Pharisee. The agreement was made. Whatever it takes, get it right. As the next chapter of my life began to unfold, bringing with it chaos and secrets, it would take a lot more to keep getting it right.

2

The Way of Secrets

"Hush, Dorothy," whispered the Tiger, "you'll ruin my reputation if you are not more discreet. It isn't what we are, but what folks think we are that counts in this world."

L. Frank Baum[1]

Some advice about secrets: it's a lot easier if you don't know them in the first place.

Alan Turing[2]

Τhis chapter can't actually be written or read. Sorry. Everything I might be tempted to write or that you might want to read is, in fact, a secret.

Secrets are meant to be secret. Secrets aren't meant to be told. At least that's what the voice tells me.

The voice holds the key to the vault filled with the secrets from long ago. To put this chapter into words on paper means I have to call the soldiers down off the wall who have been stationed there since as far back as I can remember. Their role is real, their position vital. They are the guardians.

Their role? Guard the vault! Guard the vault of secrets.

About secrets, some of them are so secret they are even secret from me.

Do you have such secrets? Ones that are so bad you keep them even from yourself? For me, the secret secrets show up on the blank pages of my life—periods of my past I literally can't remember, instances and memories that others remember vividly but I have no recollection of . . . *zero*. They are experiences tucked away safely in a place inside of me even I can't reach. In the place I call . . . the vault.

Maybe you are different. Maybe you don't have a place like this—a vault of secrets walled off and guarded to keep you safe and, most importantly, to keep the ones you love safe. Right? Isn't that why we keep secrets? Maybe you don't. Maybe you've never had to journey down *The Way of Secrets*.

For me, traveling this way started soon after the way of perfection began. They were intermingled, two paths I would walk at the same time. How does one walk two ways at once, you ask?

Easily, for these ways run side by side. Like an old dirt road with two worn-down tire tracks running parallel after years of use by dusty Chevys and Fords, perfectionism and secrets run together. I began traveling down both, the right foot in one track with the left foot in the other, separated only by the thin patch of untouched grass and wildflowers that grow in the middle.

The first time my foot stepped onto the way of secrets was soon after I was caught lying about the bubble gum.

Secret #1

I was young, about six or seven, learning and working hard to get everything right.

That evening I was supposed to be taking a bath. The tub was full, but I hadn't gotten in yet because I needed something. What I needed I don't remember, but I do remember leaving the bathroom and heading into the living room—where I saw my mom kissing someone. That someone was *not* my dad.

I remember freezing, not knowing what to do. This was a new situation, which meant it came with new rules I didn't know. When you don't know, you freeze, still, like a statue. I slowly backed out of the living room and headed to find my sister. She was older. She would know what to do.

I quickly found her and told her what I had just seen. To my surprise, she turned and looked at me with an expression I had never seen before but clearly remember. With my now-adult interpretation, I can describe the look as authoritarian, empty, and almost cold. Quickly and matter-of-factly, she said, "Forget you ever saw anything. And, Melissa, don't tell anyone."

Paralyzed, I tried to digest her words. Finally finding some unknown strength to turn and move, I headed back to the bathroom with my arms full, as I had just picked up my vault with its first secret locked deep inside.

Protection

As you are digesting the first secret, I find myself choking on the words just spoken as voices war in my head. Did that really happen? What if you made it up? How did you just make your mom look, sharing that? How can you say those things? You have so few memories of your childhood.

Back and forth my thoughts argue, exhausting me. Luckily, I can find company and solace in the words of Frederick Buechner: "When it comes to putting my own life into words, however, the doubts persist even so. Are the events I describe anything like the way they really happened?"[3]

The memory looks real, feels real. So is it real? I hope not.

I hope it's one of those images created by an angry child making up stories in her head to excuse her own bad behavior. I hope, I wish.

It's what came after the secret that can't be made up, or at least I haven't found a way to. What I can't resolve, or find another excuse for, is the change that occurred inside of me the day that first secret was put into the vault. As the door to the vault silently closed, the little girl standing in the bathroom morphed from a little girl into a protector of secrets, a protector of all.

Protector of *all*—that's a little dramatic, eh? Maybe, or maybe not. "All" included all of the major players in this little girl's world:

Her mother—protect her secret.
Her father—protect his heart.
Her sister—protect her advice and knowledge.
Her grandparents—protect their feelings.
God—protect him from seeing Mom.

Protect.
Protect.
Protect.

Earn.
Perform.
Protect.
Repeat.

Got it!

> Make the list.
> Check it twice.
> Keep your mouth shut.
> Everyone will think you're nice.

Like a good little girl, I did what I was told, and I now sit here reflecting curiously on what that day did to my soul.

I became a protector. Like the fajita steak salad I am eating right now, this truth is meatier and requires more chewing to swallow.

I became a protector. Protectors defend the weak. I can't be weak if I am to protect. I must stay strong. I must.

I can't need. I must protect—perfectly.

The framework of protection was hammered into place that day on top of the newly laid concrete foundation of perfectionism. Both pieces would prove to be important in the construction of the palace in which my heart would later live—my palace, where I got to sit on the throne as god, the protector, provider, and savior of myself. But that's a few stories away.

For now, secret #2.

Secret #2

As I ponder secret #2, I see the key master's grip tighten, and his glaring look clearly communicates he has no intention of opening the vault door again. He tempts me to dismiss this next secret as unimportant, trivial compared to the others in the vault. Yet I find myself arguing with him to open the door. Curiosity rises, as even now I don't know the consequences this secret holds. We argue back and forth, and I win.

Wait. Is this vault door opening a win?

The vault door opens and as he hands me the secret, I wonder why I am even considering telling you this. What value does revealing this secret hold?

It began in the two-story home of some family friends. The kitchen had tan walls and a rectangular table with brown, hardwood floors, or maybe it was carpet or tile. I don't really remember, but I do know the stairs to the second story were steep. I know because I sat at the top of those stairs, protecting. I was in charge of guarding a door.

At the top of the stairs was their son's rather large bedroom, or so it felt to this little version of me. The walls were dark in color, the closet door was white, and a football sat on a dusty shelf. Nothing genius in those details, eh? Maybe not, but I can't forget them, because before I was assigned to protect the door, I was allowed to play in his bedroom. He had a twin bed. I lay on the floor beside it, staring at the closet, with him on top of me. I didn't understand; I just wanted to be done. It wasn't fun. They were not happy with me because I obviously wasn't "playing" right. After they got tired of me, I was told to pull up my pants and leave—not outside the house, but outside the door—to protect, to keep the parents who were talking downstairs from walking in. I was to stand guard until those inside who knew how to play right came and got me.

I sat silently at the top of the stairs, like a good little girl, protecting, while staring down into the kitchen at four adults who were completely oblivious to what was going on behind the door at the top of the stairs.

I sat observing, trying to comprehend what I had done. Had I done bad? What had been done to me? Was I doing bad now? What did I need to do—nothing, something? I had no rules on how to navigate this new situation. I was alone.

Isn't that the challenge of secrets? You are the only company they are allowed to keep.

I just went into the kitchen for a spoonful of Ben & Jerry's Half Baked ice cream, half hoping it will bring solace to this memory in my soul. As my taste buds thank God for the delicious vanilla/chocolate/brownie ice cream yumminess, I wonder what value there was in sharing this secret.

Maybe it's to encourage you to read chapter 4, so you can avoid medicating with ice cream to soothe your soul. Maybe it's because you're a parent, and I want to encourage you to have a "door open at all times" policy for your kids. Maybe it's to acknowledge the experience for what it was, even if I still don't fully know. Maybe it's to provide you with your own opportunity to voice things that happened to you. Maybe a confusing, unclear memory lies deep within you that the Holy Spirit wants to counsel and comfort you on. Maybe it's because the secrets of the dark lose their power when they are exposed to light.

Maybe that little girl sitting alone at the top of the stairs that day just wanted someone to share her story with, and today she found enough courage to use her voice. Maybe it's the sum of all those things wrapped up together in one nicely packaged box.

That's secret #2, its memories and lessons all wrapped up. Now to secret #3.

Secret #3

Maybe secret #3 isn't really a secret. I say that as the key master stands there staring at me, with the vault open and his half-cocked expression of "Really?" At least that's what I think his expression is. He is kind of moody and hard to read at times. Maybe it's a look of disdain, since I just finished off the ice cream and didn't give him any. After all, it's his favorite flavor.

Maybe it really is "Really?" Is this really a secret? Is secret #3 *that* special to mention? As my bottom lip begins to quiver and the siren begins to blare loudly, warning that emotional overload has begun, I am aware that I don't know if it is, but it feels like it is. There is something real here in secret #3.

The secret? I hurt as a little girl—*a lot*!

Now that may not seem like a secret, because we all hurt in one way or another as kids, but for me, the protector, I couldn't hurt. I had to keep it a secret.

Like a well-done thriller movie with scenes so intense you have to look away from the screen, the memories embedded in this one secret are hard to rewatch, at least for me. You may be the scary movie, make-me-jump-out-of-my-seat, thriller-type person who has a tougher digestive system and now sits disappointed that nothing juicier was just illuminated on the screen of secret #3.

But wait. The scenes of this movie are scary, opening with a car pulling into an apartment complex with a dirty pool. I remember the pool vividly, because it was difficult to tell if it was more blue, or green, or brown—not quite the color of mold, not really the color of that toilet bowl cleaner that turns the water blue, and not the shade of mud, but combine all three and you have the color of that pool. What was most striking wasn't the color of the pool but the inability to clearly see the bottom. You could barely make out the broken chair that had long ago sunk to the bottom of the deep end. What you could see fairly clearly were the dirty objects floating in it, one of which was a baby doll's head. I remember having to walk by the pool, frightened the doll would come and get me.

The apartment complex was located in the new town we had just moved to, the town where the real pain of secret #3 began.

It was to this small, West Texas, dusty town that my dad's extremely important company had transferred him to take over a critically important store. At least it felt as if my dad thought it was *that* important. From my perspective, his job was always very important to him, *very* important. He was following in his father's footsteps, and even at a young age, I knew it was crucial for my dad to make his father proud. So we loaded up in the car, my sister, my mother, and me, and headed west with my dad to his new position. Have you been to West Texas? It's hot and dry and not much else.

Now I know some of you West Texas fans have already started forming the complaint in your head to email me, but hear me out. I like trees and mountains. There aren't many of those in West Texas. I know, there is a different type of beauty there, but beauty is in the eye of the beholder, and I struggled to find any beauty while living there. Maybe it was because I was so little, or because my little life was falling apart, or because it was so hot and the heat always killed my pet horny toads, which I caught and tried to keep alive in a shoebox.

It was hot (poor toads) and dry and difficult. The difficulties had nothing to do with the town or that part of Texas. They had to do with the dynamics of my world at the time. The fragile ecosystem of my life began to crack after eating dinner one night at Furr's, a family-favorite restaurant growing up. For those of you not familiar with Furr's, think Luby's. Furr's had yummy chocolate silk pie and square fried fish that I loved. To think about that square fried fish now is funny, because I've never seen a square fish, and I don't like fish now. But back then I loved it, maybe because it tasted like a big square French fry with tartar sauce.

One night, after eating such a square fried fish dinner, we were back home and my sister and I were sitting in the living room watching TV. My mom and dad asked us to turn the TV off (which still required walking across the room at the time) and come into the bedroom. While sitting on the bed, they informed us they were getting a divorce.

Yes, a divorce.

I don't remember the reasons they gave, but I remember them trying to make it sound positive. Like everything was going to be okay.

Why do parents do this? Make it sound positive, or better. It wasn't okay. It wasn't better. Maybe they were trying to convince themselves more than us. Who knows?

That was the beginning of the end—of many things. It was as if the umbilical cord to my dad was cut that night. That may sound strange, but I was a daddy's girl, and after the divorce, my dad was never the same. I think my mother's cheating broke his heart. I'm not saying that my dad was perfect and had no responsibility for the breakup and the divorce. But my memories of him during that time make me believe that the affair broke something in him.

I've often wondered if it broke the night of *the fight*. In case you've never lived through one, "fight nights" are much more enjoyable in the movies than in real life.

Let's set the scene for "fight night."

The Fight

My mother's boss, whom she'd been having an affair with, drove to West Texas to see my mom, and my dad found out. I remember the screaming and the punches being thrown between my dad and that man. My mother grabbed my sister and me and took us out of the apartment. With a frightened look on her face, she ran with us to the car and put us on the floor in the backseat. Before she shut the door on us, each curled up in a fetal position, she said, "Stay quiet and stay down. I will be back."

A couple of eternities seemed to pass before she came back with that still-frightened look in her eyes. She drove us to the babysitter's house, where we spent the night without her or my dad. I remember as we drove over sitting silently in the car and wondering if my dad was still alive. With nowhere safe to process the emotions, questions, panic, and fear, I did what I had learned to do best: Watch. Wait. Respond with the next "right" thing.

Protect.
Protect Mom.
Protect Dad.
Do the next right thing.

I wonder now what that next right thing was.

My memory flips to the next card in the vault drawer labeled secret #3, and I find myself in the living room of my dad's new apartment, tears streaming down his face. As he cried, he handed me a new, brown teddy bear. Near the rear of the bear was a small silver hoop that wound up a music box hidden inside the new bear. Through his tears he told me that I had to go with my mom, and he would try to see me whenever he could.

My mom was moving back to central Texas to be with "him." I remember having to let go of my dad. I remember walking down the sidewalk carrying that brown teddy bear and getting into the car. As the door slammed shut, I quickly turned around and stared out the back window screaming "I want my daddy!" as the car drove off.

A part of me has silently screamed that ever since.

Secret #4

My mother married my then-and-still-now stepfather shortly after.

Because I was little at the time, I don't remember the exact time frame of events that followed. I know we'd get packed up into the car every now and then and meet my grandparents on my dad's side. They would drive us the rest of the long way to see him, which was hard because my sister and I were crammed in the back of an old maroon Lincoln for what felt like days. (And can we just stop to note that I am a little bitter that we didn't have iPads or tablets or portable video games to keep us company during those trips that seemed to last long enough for an iceberg to form or melt or both.)

The trips were relatively regular at first, but then they became more infrequent, which was fine by me because everything had changed. My father was different. I hate to say this, but it's an important framework for later: I started being scared of my dad. He was so emotional. I couldn't calm him down. I couldn't figure out a way to protect him from him, which made me feel not safe. It made the protector feel weak, and I didn't like to feel weak.

He would pull me aside for these intense one-on-one conversations, which led to secret #4. What's said by one parent can't be heard by the other.

If your parents are divorced, then you may know this secret. As a child of divorced parents who didn't get along, I was always being told things by one parent that I wasn't supposed to tell the other—*ever*.

Secret upon secret piled up in the controlling, manipulating, tug-of-war, love-me-more-than-the-other-parent, hellish war that children of divorce are often caught in. I remember my dad telling me horrible things about my mom and why I shouldn't love her. There was one time in particular when he pulled me aside alone and said that if I loved my stepfather, or even liked him, that he would never love me again.

I am not sure words can convey the damage done to children by parents who use them as pawns in a bitter chess game of fear and control. No one wins, especially not the children.

But I was a good little soldier. I earned many more badges for my protector uniform. I worked hard to protect one side from hurting the other, and vice versa. Unfortunately, the tug-of-war proved too much, and I finally had to give up and pick sides emotionally.

I chose Mom, and I emotionally threw in the towel with my dad. The visits to see him were too hard. He was so upset, so up and down. Staying at his apartment with him and his roommate was hard. I couldn't imagine living with him; being with him was, well, confusing. And I was afraid that if I chose him, my mom wouldn't want me.

On many of our visits he went to work, and my sister and I would stay at his apartment alone. I was eight or nine, maybe; my sister was five years older. We'd walk down to the pool, which was, of course, fun for two girls. Crazy now to think we did that by ourselves. Maybe it was safe for two girls to go to the pool alone in the '80s, maybe not, but thankfully, we were safe.

Off we went. We played. We had fun, especially on the grape soda day. One day at the pool, I paused for a very important soda break. I headed to the soda machine, dropped in my change, pushed the button for a Welch's grape soda, and didn't get one. Instead, out popped an aluminum can with a plastic lid on top. When I pulled it off, I found it contained a free Welch's T-shirt and change to get another drink. It was the coolest thing in the whole world at the time.

I remember us running back to the apartment, searching everywhere to find more change. "Borrowing" what we could find, we sprinted back to the pool, dropping the round silver pieces into the vending machine in hopes of getting more shirts. We didn't get another shirt, but we did get a lot of Welch's grape soda, which was fine with me!

But back to the confusion . . .

Monkey See

The conversations my dad would try to have with me were scary and confusing. Cornered and alone, I had no tools with which to calm him down or to sort out the things he said about Mom or why work was so important that we had to stay at the apartment alone or why he didn't move back to central Texas to be closer to us. He said he loved us, yet we couldn't see him.

There was a lot of confusion in my life at the time—including experiencing cable TV for the first time. Some of you may be laughing or rolling your eyes, but growing up in my world meant three or four channels. Of those stations, my viewing was monitored, so the first time I experienced cable was eye-opening. I remember watching MTV for the first time and being mesmerized by Dire Straits's music video "Money for Nothing." The video played every hour, because there weren't many music videos back then, and I would sit and watch it over and over.

Then there was Showtime, with shows I knew we weren't allowed to watch but did. I get that kids everywhere watch cable now and blah, blah, blah. That doesn't mean it's good for them. It surely wasn't good for me. It ushered in a world I was better off not seeing or knowing about. It gave me another secret to add to my vault, but it wouldn't be big enough to qualify as secret #5. Cable TV was too small for that honor.

Secret #5

I discovered porn.

Yes, discovering porn in my father's apartment opened up Pandora's box and with it enough material to haunt and enslave me for decades.

Porn is like that. It creates this crazy web of excitement, disgust, shame, desire, curiosity, and judgment—all woven tightly together inside your soul. I know some of you have had similar experiences of discovering a poorly hidden *Playboy* magazine when you were young. You wonder whose it is, and it changes the way you see its owner. My father had a roommate. Was the porn his? Why did I want to look at it again?

If you're like me, seeing porn at an early age awoke a desire and a temptation that would be difficult to keep at bay. I would spend my remaining childhood years slipping away from my mom at a convenience or grocery store, so I could walk down the magazine aisle to take quick peeks at the plastic-wrapped magazines on the top shelf, even though you couldn't see anything except the top half of the magazine's name. What I would learn is that I loved secrets, especially *bad* secrets that no one knew. Seeing those magazines on the top shelf would bring the kind of excitement that only *bad* secrets could. My own *bad* little secret was now hidden in the vault.

Secret #6

Lying next to #5 in the vault is secret #6, which is a bad secret for a good girl growing up to have. Sharing a secret like this requires breaking many family and societal rules.

The secret? I didn't like my stepfather, at all, which for a good Christian girl is not good to say. As you well-mannered, socially trained individuals probably know, you don't tell people, "I don't like you." Not behind their backs and definitely not to their faces. Instead, you hide, shade, and portray versions of truth you think other people want to see and hear. As a perfectionist, I did this well. I was very, very good at playing the part of the perfect daughter in the perfect family when I needed to. But behind the scenes, things weren't perfect, and I didn't like him. Not. One. Bit.

After all, I blamed him for my parents' divorce, which broke my heart. I knew my mom had done wrong, but I blamed him. I saw the part he played in splitting my parents apart.

He seemed mean and controlling—like a dictator, always wanting what *he* wanted. At least it seemed so to me, as he always made my mom cry. The way she served him made me mad. The chores and the ways he expected me to do them made me mad as well. Maybe his requests were extreme, or maybe my feelings were. As a child, it's hard sometimes to know what is true.

Instead, you only know what *feels* true. All of it *felt* true, and my stepfather didn't *feel* safe—or good. Why do I share this secret now? Because having a father figure step into your life who, from your vantage point, fails at being a good father affects you. It only pads the stack of paper listing all the reasons it's not safe to trust men.

This helps me understand the something that is missing in me.

Something Missing

There are two perfectly placed trees about ten yards away from the back porch of the house I've been writing at the past few days. The house is an older home, a small house that sits on about two hundred acres with a pond, a zipline, two deer feeders, and some of the most beautiful bluebonnets I've seen in a while. There's also a small creek on the property that you can walk to and is wonderful to sit by.

There are two small bunnies that come up to play and forage at about six every evening on the meadow past the two big trees. Early this morning, while drinking my first cup of coffee, about eight fawns came and played on the hill to the right of the pond. Their youth and vitality and the way they frolicked and played warmed my soul as much as my two-spoonfuls-of-sugar-and-cream coffee did.

Now if only I had a hammock. The two trees are a perfect distance apart, and the owners of the property installed two metal brackets in the trees for that purpose, which makes the whole situation a frustrating tease, like certain areas of my life have been.

Have you ever felt as if you were missing something important—not in your life, but missing in you? As if you came into the world without the necessary hardware or software needed to enjoy life like others around you? Like that big empty space between the two trees where a hammock should be. I've spent decades feeling as though there was a big empty space inside of me, like something was missing—because there was.

This missing piece of me was stolen by secret #7 and secret #8.

For me, it was not having the hardware and tools to navigate relationships with boys or men. When it came to talking or relating to them, I felt as if we were from different planets, like they were from Mars and I was from Venus. Funny? (For those of you who haven't read the great book *Men Are from Mars, Women Are from Venus*, you might have missed that little joke!)

Watching the way other girls interacted with boys, I knew something was off. It seemed they had an instruction manual I didn't, as if I'd missed the issue of *Seventeen* magazine (back in the '90s) that covered the ten best ways to talk to boys. I just didn't know how to do it. I felt scared, unattractive, stupid, and nauseated.

Like a saltwater fish accidently put in a freshwater tank, I'd try to talk to a boy but looked more like a flopping, drowning fish that couldn't breathe. That's how it felt talking to boys. It felt suffocating. Decades later, it often still does. When trying to talk to certain gentlemen, I still can't do it right.

Remember, the rules are always in effect, even when talking to boys.

Do it right.
Keep your mouth shut.
Protect.
Stay strong.

Secret #7

Talking with boys made me feel weak. I wasn't allowed to be weak.

This suffocating saltwater fish would try to navigate the turbulent and scary waters of dating, but I was ill-equipped because of what I was missing.

My toolbox of necessary dating tools tipped over during the divorce and was shaken out in the emotional aftermath and stomped on by the abandonment of my father. It was a slower abandonment than most, emotional at first because the divorce destroyed his ability to keep it together around me. The physical abandonment heightened when he moved away to Colorado, which meant visits happened once a year, if that. Then he remarried. Like every good Cinderella story with a stepmother, this princess wasn't wanted around.

The relationship with my father slipped through my hands and into someone else's, like a wad of cash at a Black Friday sale. I was no longer needed or wanted, or so I felt. But I was tough and strong. I was the protector—a soldier who could soldier on. With the wounds of abandonment hidden deep underneath my already worn-out uniform, I continued on.

It would take thirty years for the silent secret #7 to emerge, which would shed light on the emptiness of my toolbox. This secret was hidden deep in the inner cell of the vault where secret secrets were kept.

It's called a repressed memory. Have you experienced one? I pray not. Repressed memories are memories kept locked away in the subconscious part of the brain, because to remember them would be too painful. Not remembering them is a self-preservation strategy built into us by God. We are able to remember them only when we are healthy enough to deal with the emotions of them. "This is why physical and sexual abuse victims sometimes lose memory of great segments of time: keeping the memories would be too catastrophic to the individual."[4]

The secret memory surfaced a year or so ago when I was doing some therapeutic inner healing work. The event? I was eight or nine, in my dad's apartment, in a bedroom. The details are graphic and I won't share them here. I cannot see the man's face.

Unlike the sexual abuse of secret #7, in which some details remain unclear, I can remember every detail of secret #8.

Secret #8

Secret #8 involves a slamming screen door. I was twenty, and the sexual abuse that occurred that day was real. The effects were tragic in the freedom and joy they stole. In fact, the effects still ripple across the surface of my life. No, they don't rock my boat like they used to. But every now and then I can feel the difference in the waters that should be still.

As I type, I can see every detail like it was yesterday, but some details in this story can't be shared without permission from the perpetrator, which I don't have.

It's true. I actually did brave my fears and reach out to the man and ask if I could share this story. Yes, I still know him. He could be a family member, friend, deacon, or famous person from Hollywood. Who he is doesn't really matter. His answer does though. As you would expect, he said no to my request for permission. That hurt.

It hurt so much that I couldn't write about it at all yesterday and instead tried to navigate my anger and emotions with a good run, a box of Kleenex, and finishing off the pint of ice cream I swore to myself I wasn't going to touch. Yes, I admit it, I want this secret out in the open.

I have shared this secret with those whom I can. It took me a long time to do so. I kept this secret locked inside until I was twenty-six. If you've done the math, you realize I went six years without uttering a word of the molestation. It often takes time for victims to heal enough to be able to use their voice.

This is one reason I'd like to see our laws changed. Depending on the situation, you may have only up to five years before the statute of limitations has passed. But the more painful the abuse—emotional, physical, or sexual—the longer it could take for someone to be healed enough or feel safe enough to share.

I'd also like to see the church change to where a perpetrator has a safe place to use their voice. Yes, I said *perpetrator*. One of the main reasons I wanted to share this story is so that the individual who preyed on me that day would have the opportunity to use his voice and, in doing so, experience freedom and grace. He deserves grace just as much as I do.

Most statistics quote that one in three women have been sexually abused or molested at some point. Some say one in four. Either way, there are a lot of wounded women out there, which means there are also a lot of hurt, broken men doing these tragic deeds. This makes me wonder if the church ever feels like a safe place to go for someone who has made this kind of mistake.

Actually, I don't wonder, I know. One of the primary reasons this man gave when refusing permission was that he didn't want people in his church to know. Does it hurt you as much to read as it does me to type? The one place a predator should be able to go for help and restoration should be a church.

Wounded abusers deserve an opportunity to experience love and healing at the foot of the cross. It has taken me a long time to come to this place. For many years, I plotted and dreamed about how to repay this abuser and others for what they stole from me on those days. It hasn't been easy to reach a point of forgiving him or other men for their sins. Difficult, yes. But possible. It's easier now as I am keenly aware that someone else has forgiven me of mine. As you will read in the next chapters, God is able, and his specialty is the impossible things of life.

For now, though, my abuser's secret is his to keep, which I understand. I too spent so many years believing that keeping secrets keeps you safe.

Magicians

Isn't it amazing, the ability we have to lie to ourselves?

Our pride tells us that not only can we keep the secrets but also, in doing so, they won't affect us. We lock them up in a vault and, without realizing it, enslave ourselves. As Buechner said, "I not only have my secrets, I am my secrets. You are yours."[5] Our secrets become our masters, dictating who we are allowed to become as we shift and shade every part of our lives away from the secrets. Like a master magician, skilled in the art of misdirection, we manipulate our lives with every bit of effort and energy, working to draw attention away from the truth we can't allow anyone to see. For those who have mastered the way of secrets, it is easy to believe that no one knows. But someone always knows. We aren't as good at keeping things hidden as we think we are.

One day, everyone will know. Jesus said so. Hear his words as he addresses his disciples, warning them of the Pharisees, the religious leaders who were the masters of secrets: "Everything that is hidden will be shown, and everything that is secret will be made known. What you have said in the dark will be heard in the light, and what you have whispered in an inner room will be shouted from the housetops" (Luke 12:2–3 NCV).

Scary? If you're hiding something, it is. Let me ask, What are you hiding? How's that working for you? You're tired, aren't you? Keeping secrets is just that—exhausting.

King David can relate: "When I kept silent, my bones wasted away through my groaning all day long" (Ps. 32:3). For those not familiar with King David, he was known in the Bible as a man after God's own heart. But he was a king with plenty of secrets—family secrets, bad little secrets. He impregnated Bathsheba and then had her faithful warrior husband, Uriah, killed. I'd be tired carrying around secrets of adultery and murder too!

David didn't stay enslaved and exhausted by his secrets though. He confessed and shared them and found peace and joy.

> Then I acknowledged my sin to you
>   and did not cover up my iniquity.
> I said, "I will confess
>   my transgressions to the LORD."
> And you forgave
>   the guilt of my sin. . . .

You are my hiding place;
  you will protect me from trouble
  and surround me with songs of deliverance. . . .
Many are the woes of the wicked,
  but the Lord's unfailing love
  surrounds the one who trusts in him.
Rejoice in the Lord and be glad, you righteous;
  sing, all you who are upright in heart! (Ps. 32:5, 7,
    10–11 NIV)

Let's pause and learn from David. He stayed silent about his secrets and he suffered. He confessed and found freedom, protection, and joy.

Silence leads to suffering. Confession leads to joy. Two different paths—I wonder which one you are on.

Is the path you're on leading you toward greater daily joy? May I share something I've learned? Joy can only come when we are fully known. That moment when the horrible, deplorable, sickening, I-can't-believe-I-did-that self is known and still loved is the moment we can experience real joy.

Don't agree? Let me see if Buechner can convince you.

That what we hunger for perhaps more than anything else is to be known in our full humanness, and yet that is often just what we also fear more than anything else. It is important to tell at least from time to time the secret of who we truly and fully are—even if we tell it only to ourselves—because otherwise we run the risk of losing track of who we truly and fully are and little by little come to accept instead the highly edited version which we put forth in hope that the world will find it more acceptable than the real thing. It is important to tell our secrets too because it makes it easier that way to see where we have been in our lives and where we are going. It also makes it easier for other people to tell us a secret or two of their own, and exchanges like that have a lot to do with what being a family is all about and what being human is all about. Finally, I suspect that it is by entering that deep place inside us where our secrets are kept that we come perhaps closer than we do anywhere else to the One who, whether we realize it or not, is of all our secrets the most telling and the most precious we have to tell.[6]

Be Real

Here's the challenge for this chapter: be *fully known*.

Start with yourself. Take a step out of denial and stop the magical manipulating act in which you keep yourself from looking at you. Be real with yourself and someone else. Yes, I know that it's tough to be real with someone else. We will discuss the challenges that come with that in chapter 7. Pursuing authentic relationships can be scary, but it is the most horrible yet life-changing truth that "darkness always needs the light of unconditional love to give up its secrets."[7]

Take it from someone who spent too long walking the way of secrets: you weren't meant to walk through life carrying a vault. You were meant to run, to dance, to dream.

It's difficult to dream when living in the barren land of denial and deception. It's a lonely place to carry your vault, especially if a monster grows inside.

3

The Way of the Monster

I am telling a story of two lives. They have nothing to do with
each other: oil and vinegar, a river running beside a canal, Jekyll
and Hyde. Fix your eye on either and it claims to be the sole truth.

C. S. Lewis[1]

I miss college. Then again, I don't. Some of the best days of my
life occurred there, and some of the worst.

I've often wondered if this is true for most people fortunate
enough to attend college right out of high school. It's a Jekyll/
Hyde, yin/yang type of experience. The highest of highs followed
by the lowest of lows—all experiences captured perfectly by the
words of Dickens:

It was the best of times, it was the worst of times, it was the age
of wisdom, it was the age of foolishness, it was the epoch of belief, it was the epoch of incredulity, it was the season of Light, it
was the season of Darkness, it was the spring of hope, it was the
winter of despair, we had everything before us, we had nothing

before us, we were all going direct to Heaven, we were all going direct the other way.[2]

All Planned Out

Life for this perform, protect, keep-it-quiet, do-it-right, "perfect" Christian girl at the private Christian university I attended was just that—the best and the worst of times.

I sailed through my freshman year, made good grades, and made some of the best friends I thought I could ever have. I even stuck my toe into the scary waters of the college dating scene, where the stakes were high because your next first date could actually be with the man you were going to marry, or at least I hoped that was what would someday happen.

I decided to major in home economics, as the thought of getting paid to bake chocolate chip cookies all day with high school students seemed like a good one. This was also a strategic move, as I knew it would help pad the marriage potential résumé. What good Christian boy wouldn't want to marry someone with Betty Crocker skills?

I had it all planned out. I would date someone who was going into youth ministry and marry him right after college. This would allow me the opportunity to do youth ministry as well, since the very conservative denomination I grew up in didn't allow females on church staff other than as secretaries. I hated filing and typing. Actually, anything related to desk work or a cubicle can easily cause me to break out in a rash.

I wanted to marry a youth minister. If, for some reason, my plan didn't succeed accordingly, I would teach after graduating until I found the future Mr. Perfect Christian to marry. That was the brilliant plan I had scheduled in my 1990s day planner.

My freshman year went according to plan. It was filled with fun, and there was no need for serious dating yet. I was saving that for my junior year, in which I would begin to date in earnest for twelve to eighteen months, spend one year engaged, and then marry within three to nine months of graduating. It was going to be perfect, the best of times. I had it all planned out.

The problem was I wasn't a good planner. (I'm still not. I hate details and schedules. I'm a fly-by-the-seat-of-my-pants-type gal. For you Myers-Briggs fans, I am an ENFP. No thank you to planning or details. And can being on time be optional? It's really a challenge for me. I like freedom and flexibility.) But back then I had a plan, and it was going to be great.

All was on schedule, and then it happened. The monster came out.

For some of you, the word *monster* might bring to mind images of Frankenstein or Hannibal Lecter. Others might see Sully or Mike Wazowski, or even Darth Vader, or maybe someone you know more personally—a relative or your mother-in-law.

Whatever you picture, the image of a monster can range from a fluffy, overstuffed animal you want to cuddle to the vilest of characters that Hollywood can conjure up.

My monster was different yet the same.

Monsters

I wonder if you've ever had a monster, not for a pet but in you, part of you. You had no idea where it came from and, like a small child trying to walk a hyper Great Dane, had no hope of controlling it. I didn't know people had monsters. Growing up in a conservative Christian church, I never saw stories of transformation, resurrection, or redemption. Everyone I knew had it all together. No one had monsters back then.

Monsters are smart and can talk you into anything. They talk you into that one drink when you've sworn you'll never open a bottle again. They cause you to overeat again and again and again. They show up at the store, convincing you to buy that irrelevant-must-have thing while blinding you to the insurmountable mountain of debt crushing your hopes and your real dreams. They give you permission to live in that cesspool of jealousy and bitterness. They love to swim there. They entice you to search out illuminated screens with images of pornography, enslaving you to secrecy and shame. They hide in pills. They hide in a bowl of unmonitored M&Ms. They hide in shades of gray. Monsters live everywhere.

I wish I had known that then. Thinking that you're the only one with a monster can be a lonely way to live. That's how I felt when my monster reared its ugly head. Alone. With no one to talk to and no one who would understand.

It appeared slowly and quietly, almost friendly, as all monsters do. They rarely jump out fully into your life. No, they are more strategic and manipulative. Monsters are very, very smart. They are sly and subtle. Like cockroaches, they usually come out at night.

It happened one night in college. I was there as a friend, thinking that hanging out and chatting were what normal friends do. If I've ever had a struggle in life, it's been discerning what normal people do.

Even though I have an older sister and had great girlfriends in high school, I felt different from other girls. There were so many rules I didn't get: how to dress, what to say, what not to say, how to tweeze eyebrows or help someone pick out an outfit for her big first date. I would sit mesmerized, watching them interact with each other. You'd never have known I was so insecure. I was a complete professional of "observe, analyze, and do the right thing." I knew how to blend in, even while my insides felt like the ugly duckling or the odd man out.

On this particular night, one moment we were friends, and the next, the monster awakened and life in hell began. She started touching me. Completely horrified, I lay there, paralyzed. I couldn't understand what was happening, and I didn't know what I was supposed to do. I remained frozen until it stopped and she left my room.

Sometimes stories of the past are like car wrecks. Rather than staring at the scene, it's better for everyone if you keep looking forward and drive on by. That's what I tried to do after that night. Even though I was completely aware that what had happened was wrong, I tried to shut it out and drive on by. After all, what was I to do? She was a dear friend. What would she say if I confronted her? I didn't want to hurt her feelings or upset her, so I defaulted to the things I knew how to do.

Perform . . . continue being a good friend.
Protect . . . her feelings. Don't say a word to her or anyone else.
Repeat.

I didn't say anything, not a word. We hung out again, with nothing happening. Then another night, something did. Nothing, then something. Something, then nothing. I don't remember how long this went on. I only remember that at one point my reaction went from disgust at being touched to no disgust. All the while, confusion, panic, and fear radiated in my life as I tried to understand what was going on and what I needed to do.

To understand my confusion, I need to frame the early '90s for you. Ellen hadn't come out of the closet and Katy Perry hadn't "Kissed a Girl." I don't remember even hearing about the concept, let alone knowing anyone who was gay. It wasn't portrayed on TV or fought over in politics. It hadn't in any way infiltrated my little fishbowl of a world. I knew in my entire being that it was not okay, and the fact that it was never talked about only magnified that awareness. It was wrong, and I knew it.

So here I am, experiencing something I'd never heard about with someone I cared about. I couldn't understand why she would do something like this or why I would keep responding the way I did, both physically and emotionally. All I knew was that I couldn't say anything, especially to her. It would hurt her. Protectors can't hurt people, especially when they are struggling. It goes against our rules.

The web began spinning, entangling me in something I couldn't label or understand. I only knew that it had to be hidden. My biggest secret ever was now concealed in my vault. I hated it, and I had to hide it.

But somewhere in the middle of hating it, I started liking it and wanting more, which is a common trait of monsters. They *always* want more.

It was the best of times. I was climbing the social ladder. I was making good grades and going on dates with cute boys. I was friends with popular people. Life couldn't be better.

And it was the worst of times. The monster living in me made me do things I didn't want to do and didn't understand. One thing was very clear to me though. I knew God hated me for what I was doing.

I was one person living two lives: the good Christian girl dating guys and working the social scene, the bad girl doing vile things with her friend. I felt like two people: Melissa and the monster. I was trying to keep one alive and silently kill the other.

But the monster wouldn't die.

I begged God to kill it, to take it away. I'd lie on the floor of my room, crying night after night, playing "She Talks to Angels" by the Black Crowes. Over and over again, I'd beg God to do whatever it took to remove it. I believed he could. I couldn't understand why he wouldn't. I assumed it must have been me—I was the problem. So I'd lie there crying, begging, trying to find reasons not to kill myself. If God wasn't going to take the same-sex desire away, the only solution was suicide. But killing myself would hurt Mom. I had to protect Mom. I cried every night, stuck. I couldn't keep doing it—living two lives.

You probably know this all too well yourself: duplicitous living sucks.

Love It, Hate It

James, the half brother of Jesus, warns the disciples that the double-minded man is unstable in all he does (James 1:8). Double-minded best described me: one girl with what felt like two souls.

With all of my being, I wanted to be a good Christian girl and live the way that I knew I should. I tried. I'd swear I wasn't going to talk to her or let those things happen again. I even secretly went to an Exodus meeting hoping to get help. (Exodus was a controversial but well-meaning organization dedicated to helping people find freedom from their same-sex desires and struggles. The one meeting I bravely attended merely succeeded in scaring the crap out of me, and I determined I'd never go to anything like that again. I'd figure out a way to do it on my own.) Yet over and over I'd fail.

I would read Paul's words in Romans, hoping to find comfort from the apostle, because he seemed to understand my struggle: "For I do not understand my own actions. For I do not do what I want, but I do the very thing I hate" (Rom. 7:15). I would scream out, "Yes! I know! I don't want to do what I am doing either! What do I do about it, Paul?"

The silence that followed was stifling. I would sit for hours, pondering the struggle that never seemed to end.

One life was good and right; the other life was bad but would make me feel so good, so alive.

Isn't it funny how the monster can do that? It makes you feel alive even as it leads you to death. Consider the story of Jeff in *Hiding from Love*:

> Jeff learned that he was to experience only positive truths about himself. Feeling like a double agent, he was split down the middle. There was his idealized perfect self, with an adoring fan club of church friends and family. And there was his secret self, where he felt "bad"—but alive. Even so, he hated this aspect of himself. "All I ever thought about was all the people who looked up to me—how disappointed and hurt they'd be if it came out."[3]

Intervention

Like Jeff, I'd never felt as alive as I did when doing "bad," but I couldn't say anything about it. I couldn't ask for help. My perfect self couldn't imagine my friends finding out. How could I put into words for someone else something that I couldn't explain to myself? I played over and over in my head the horror that would come if my monster was discovered by my friends.

Then the nightmare became a reality. Some friends found out about my struggle, and the intervention began.

Have you ever had an intervention? Been caught in the middle of your greatest sin and called out on it by a group of people? It's awful. You could have filled the Grand Canyon with the amount of shame I felt, sitting in a room while being handed an ultimatum—go to counseling or someone would tell my mom. Though petrified of going to a counselor, the choice was easy. Mom couldn't have handled this news. *I must protect Mom.*

Luckily, there were only a few weeks of that school year left. I went to counseling for the first time in my life and made it through finals. Somehow in the middle of it all, I managed not to kill myself, because it was very tempting to end it all. The pain was so great.

I made it to the end of the semester. I made it out alive. I couldn't drive away fast enough from that college town as I headed home for the summer. I had a youth ministry intern position lined up that I had to awkwardly cancel the week before, citing a "personal issue." This was a difficult phone call to make as I loved working with teens, and that summer I was going to have an opportunity to intern with a guy I'd had a huge crush on the previous two years. (It's depressing the opportunities for life that monsters steal from us as they lead us toward death.)

While driving home, I swore I was done. That monster was not going to control me anymore. I wasn't going to let it steal another moment or opportunity with a great guy or a great job. I was done. I had reached a new level of hatred for my monster. As Jesus said, "No one can serve two masters. Either you will hate the one and love the other, or you will be devoted to the one and despise the other" (Matt. 6:24 NIV). I despised my monster.

For some of you, the pain of your life is so tough right now that it seems easier to die than to live. Will you hold on? Will you reach out and let someone know you're hurting and in a tough place? If it's a lonely season and you don't have anyone to reach out to, will you call a local church or counselor and give God a chance to bring you relief and help? I know how dark some seasons can be, but there is hope—God is not done working in your life.

Conquer It All

I spent the summer "getting my head on straight" and working at a Christian bookstore. After the summer detox, I headed back to school ready to conquer the world. At least, that was what I told myself as I made the five-hour trip back. The pep talk had to work. It was the year I had to conquer everything. Many people were relying on me. I had important officer positions in organizations and social scenes that I was involved in. I was president of this and codirector of that. I couldn't be two people and get things done.

Luckily, the monster stayed in his cage, so still and silent I thought he was dead, which was good. I needed him dead. I had things to do. I was important. I had responsibilities. I had to keep it together. And I did. It was great. I dated boys. I led. I made the dean's list. I was nominated for homecoming queen. I was normal!

At least I hoped I was. I prayed I was.

Hurt by Church

My senior year flew by. Most of my friends graduated, but since I changed my major late in the game (to exercise science, which would allow me to teach and coach basketball), I needed an extra year.

It was different being a fifth-year senior, especially at a small university. Having done everything there was to do the previous year, I had an odd feeling knowing it was someone else's turn to be important. I was a has-been. I was known but not needed. My ego hated it.

I made up my mind it was going to be a good year anyway. I had been offered a job I thought was important. This gave me another arena to work and achieve in, while I tidied up the loose ends keeping me from walking that stage and getting that ever-so-important diploma.

Yes, this was going to be a good year, which it was—until it wasn't. Looking back on that year, I see it was like a cheap bottle of wine, one you'd just as soon leave on the shelf. That was the year I was wounded by the church.

No, I don't mean the entire church rallied around and conspired to hurt this seemingly unimportant college kid. Nothing so dramatic. But sadly, what sometimes happens is that people proudly wearing the label "Christian," "churchgoer," or even "church friend" on their chests show up more like Judas than Jesus. This place once thought of as safe instantly changes. Sins committed by a few change the identity and the label. The safest place to be becomes not safe at all, which is tragic and all too painful.

For me, the pain was inflicted by church friends. *Betrayal*, *deceit*, and *abandonment* are three words that come to mind when I travel back to that time. Were you ever wounded by a church friend? Did you ever suffer the pains of spiritual abuse?

Yes, spiritual abuse. For those of you not familiar with the term or its effects, it's abuse committed "under the banner of spirituality. It can be subtle or painfully loud—anything from unquestioned pastoral authority, to practices of shaming members if they don't fulfill religious expectations, to badmouthing members who have left."[4] These are just a few of the things people sometimes do while wearing their Sunday best.

While the incident mentioned above wouldn't fit the definition of spiritual abuse, I have experienced it at other times within the church. You're judged, shamed, blamed, and dismissed when *your* Sunday best is a mess because your identity and sexuality have you all turned around. Or you're trying to walk down a new path and let God be the one to define your identity, and the judgmental comments come. Or you get the cold shoulder and silent you're-not-welcome-here stare that unfortunately many church people are all too good at. It's painful.

If those church members only knew . . . (Maybe you're one of them. Maybe you've judged, shamed, slandered, or slammed your spiritual authority down on the head of some wayward sinner trying to get them to fall back in line. Maybe you've made it clear that in your church no gay, struggling, addicted, or tattooed people are welcome. I hope not, because Jesus came to save those people too, and it hurts when "in the name of Jesus" the church doors get slammed in your face.)

But I am not free to judge either. What I've learned now from my immaturity then is that church people are still in-process too, whether they be the pastor, priest, Sunday school teacher, smiling greeter, or as in my story, church friends. There may be wolves among the sheep, but there are still more sheep than wolves, and they are protected by a very powerful shepherd. Most Christ-followers are just trying to navigate this war zone of a world without getting blown to bits. So who am I not to offer grace? Especially inside the doors of the church.

Oh, but I was so young then. So young.

My personal rights were violated, and I wanted someone to play the villain, so I could justify my desire to run away, which I did. The church, full of its sinners, wasn't safe for me, so I was done. I'd keep God around, but his people and his church—he could have both, thank you very much. I might still attend church, but only to check the box. I was done trying to live my faith.

Wounded, I set out to find some fun.

New Friends

Have you ever made new friends who were completely the opposite of your old friends? It's a weird experience, but I did it. I ditched the "good girls" who loved Jesus and did all the right things, because pretty is as pretty does. Freshly wounded, I had no desire for pretty or good or anything resembling it. Misery loves company, so I found new company.

Looking back, I can now see that many of my new friends were as miserable in their lives as I was in mine. But they were exciting because they weren't so concerned with being good.

Some drank. Others smoked. They told inappropriate jokes. They made fun of people. They had fun. I had fun with them.

I needed some fun.

Sometimes it seems the only way to get through life is to distract yourself from it, which is what I did those last few months of school. I spent the last ticks of the college clock paving the new way for my next season of life, the new way in which I would live—*medicated*.

4

The Way of Medicating

Numbing the pain for a while will make it worse when you finally feel it.

J. K. Rowling[1]

I like to run. I know, for some of you, running isn't your thing. For some, movement requiring effort of any kind is out as well, especially if it is accompanied by the slight chance of pain, or worse, the possibility of sweat. Ugh. Me, I am a little bit weird. I like both.

I like the feeling of tired, spent muscles and rings of sweat left on a shirt. I am not a multimarathon-type person—I don't have 26.2 stickers on the back of my Tahoe—but I am good friends with people who do. They do crazy things such as run the Grand Canyon rim to rim, and they have logged more marathons than I've completed 5Ks. I admire their dedication and discipline, and someday I might take the challenge to complete more than the half marathon I've run.

For now, I am a casual runner who laces up her running shoes and hits the pavement or the trails whenever she can. It's in that shoe-pounding, Spotify-blaring, thirty- to forty-five-minute span of time that I am able to get away from it all. Life gets pounded out of my mind by the pounding of my shoes and the beat-thumping bass in my headphones. Not that it is always bass pumping through my headphones. Sometimes I listen to podcasts or worship music or even classical music. What's playing doesn't really matter. It's simply in being outside, pounding the miles, that life seems to disappear for a while. Sometimes I need that escape from life.

If I am honest, I am addicted to running. I am addicted to escape. I am addicted to running away from my problems. I like to run from them as far as possible. I am a classic avoider, and this run-avoid-hide mentality really got traction in my life when I stepped off the stage of my college graduation with my diploma in hand. I grabbed it and ran as fast as I could away from that college town and the trail left behind, strewn with the pieces of my shattered heart. That may sound dramatic, but that last year was devastating. I felt so wounded by people who said they loved me, people who said they loved God. I needed to get out of there. I needed a change.

New Me, Old Me

I ran to a place where no one knew my name to start a new life.

I moved to a big city in Texas, full of hope at the start of my adult life. I found a great teaching job in a great district and a nice little apartment near a trendy part of town right by a lake where I could run and bike. New things, new people, new surroundings, new opportunities to create the life I wanted with no one around me who had known me before. I could be anyone and do anything, and I was going to do just that.

I had all the pieces to the perfect puzzle. The only piece I hadn't factored into my perfect equation was, well, me. As I set off on this new adventure, I didn't factor in that I was wounded. Wounded people don't adventure well.

My hurting heart needed healing before it could begin to truly enjoy the new surroundings, but who has time for healing? Like many athletes, I thought I could walk off the emotional injury I had just endured. Unfortunately, I didn't realize how injured my heart was. It was broken, not just sprained. My broken heart couldn't trust, and you can't go very far with a heart unable to trust.

When you are wounded, you feel like nothing, like you don't matter. It's scary because when you think you're nothing you will do *anything* to feel like something. That's how I left college, feeling and subconsciously believing I was nothing—nothing important, nothing worth fighting for. Wounds will take you down one of two paths, but never both: either you walk the tough trail toward true healing, or you search out the easy way of medicating. I set out skipping along the easy path.

I began to medicate my pain by becoming somebody. Through work, I thought I could do just that. I threw myself into my first year of teaching and coaching determined to be the best. I quickly learned that, yes, work helped to ease the pain. I could coach, win a game, be applauded, and the ointment of acceptance and approval would soothe the infected cracks in my heart. Like a thin layer of Neosporin spread over a cut, however, the ointment of approval would last only so long before I would need it again. What was convenient was that in coaching there was always another game to win. I was in a great district with great kids and, of course, I was a great coach (wink, wink), so the wins kept coming. The temporary ointment was applied again and again. I was being noticed. This lowly, first-year, middle school teacher was noticed by coaches higher up the coaching chain. I dreamed of promotions up that ladder. Maybe one day I would be the head coach of a big high school and have other coaches working under me. For now, I would get whatever ointment I could. Like a crack addict hustling for his next fix, I worked hard to earn the next win on the court or in the classroom that would provide the next dose of praise my heart needed. The praise would come and the pain would cease. I was hooked.

Are you hooked on the drug of work too? Do you use work to escape? Does the praise that comes along with the promotion fill in the cracks left by the "you aren't good enough" message carved on your heart long ago? Do you sacrifice your body or your peace of mind for the false security of working just a little bit longer? What do you have to do to earn your attaboys? What do you have to compromise? Is it worth it? While you might be arguing the benefits, I ask you, What's the cost? What is medicating your heart with work really costing you?

When I wasn't working twelve- to sixteen-hour days, I made time to go to church. After all, going to church was what I was *supposed* to do. But when you feel wounded and betrayed by church people, the normal routine of going to church changes. While I was growing up and in college, not only did I go to church, but I was also a part of the church. I was known. I was involved. I served. I led.

Attending church wounded was different. Like an abused dog afraid to be touched again, I would quietly sneak in the church doors right as the service started and leave as quickly as I could afterward. I would sing a few songs, listen to some old man in a suit speak, and leave having spoken to no one. I could check the box that I went and so satisfy that part of my head that said I should go. Walking through the doors every Sunday so guarded made it impossible for anything that was said to penetrate the shield of protection around my heart and soul. This weekly routine left me starving for love and friendship. Thankfully, with the new friends I was beginning to make through work, I didn't have to feel alone. In fact, through coaching, I not only made new friends but also discovered a whole new world I'd never known.

My monster loved this new world.

In

I think it is fascinating that despite how long man has been on earth, scientists and biologists are still discovering new species of plants and animals. Take the new glass frog species, *Hyalino-batrachium dianae*, recently discovered in Chile. It is a popular discovery because the little green frogs resemble the one and only Kermit the Frog. They were never before seen but are now very well-known—a hidden species in a known world, unknown but then found.

Like the unknown world I discovered when I bought a scooter. In 2008, to fight soaring gas prices, I bought a supercool scooter that got eighty miles to the gallon. Okay, so it wasn't really cool at all, and most people called it a moped and laughed at it. It did get eighty miles to the gallon, though, and I thought it was fun to drive.

What was shocking to me was the secret hand signs I would get from motorcycle riders on the road. As a car driver, I had no idea those on motorcycles did this, but as a scooter driver, my eyes were opened, and I was welcomed into this secret world, well, kind of.

You see, when two bikers pass each other, they might greet each other with hand signs such as the Two-Finger Flip or the Big One. These are common greetings made with the left hand to politely greet the oncoming biker and, in a simple way, to even say, "Nice bike." Not all bikers greet one another, and some greet only those with similar type bikes. As a scooter driver in the motorcycling world, you don't always get greeted. It's like showing up at the country club with a set of rented golf clubs from the '80s and wearing tennis shoes. They might let you play, but then again, they might not.

Sometimes I got let in the club by a kind Harley driver who politely flipped up the two fingers to say hi. Never was I greeted by a Japanese rocket driver as he passed by, probably wishing I would go back to reading in the library or some other geeky, scooter-driving activity.

Like discovering the unknown world of motorcycle greeting, entering the world of coaching unlocked a world and culture I'd never known existed: the gay world.

I'll Help Them

While coaching, I made friends with coaches who were gay. Please don't read that sentence and stereotype that all coaches are this or all _____ are that. Stereotypes help no one. The point is that a new job in a new city afforded me new perspectives. In the old world I lived in, no one was out of the closet. That's how it was back then. No one came out, and the gay people I met talked in secret code and were very careful when and where and how they were seen in public, especially when out with their "roommate."

For this "good girl" who thought her monster had suffocated and died, learning that some of the people she knew had "roommates" and were "family" was an eye-opening experience. Not only that, it was exciting. They were fun. They laughed. I laughed when I was with them. They didn't take themselves so seriously. They weren't bad people. In fact, I found a lot in common with them: a love of coaching, sports, the outdoors, and travel. They were protective of each other. They knew how to live out community. Most wanted to live a happy life and retire so they could play more golf or spend more time at the lake.

It was while hanging out with them that the monster began to roar again. I tried to shove it back in its cage. I knew the gay lifestyle was wrong. I wanted to get married, have a family, and be "normal." That's who I was. I wasn't gay like them.

I told myself I was spending time with them to help them grow closer to God (which is comical, or maybe just sad, as I look back on it now). Trying not to do the thing you really want to do while spending time with the people doing it obviously doesn't work. It was like being an egg dropped into a pan of hot bacon grease and trying not to fry. I quickly began to sizzle.

I fought it hard though, and thankfully, I had help. In the summers, I left and headed to Colorado, where I got to live my dream job as a backpacking guide. Have you ever had a dream job? A job so perfect that it used every gift you've been given while letting you live in the perfect setting and work with the perfect people? I know, sounds impossible, but for me it happened those summers I worked as a guide for a faith-based outfitter in Colorado. As guides, we would take groups on five-day hiking trips and help them grow closer as a group and closer to God. On the weekends, we would play and have fun exploring the rest of Colorado. It was the perfect job. It was up in those mountains that something in me came alive. This something would prove pivotal a decade down the road.

Unfortunately, as every hiker knows, you can't stay on top of the mountain forever. At some point, you have to hike back down. This would prove true each summer when July rolled into August, and I would make that solemn trip back to Texas and come face-to-face with the valley of my soul.

Like a hamster on a wheel, I would cycle through the same rhythm for the next few years. Meet a guy in the summer. Try to continue dating him during the year. At some point in the year, meet someone else while coaching and hear my monster roar. Try to ignore, silence, suffocate, and kill the monster. Throw even more energy into work. Try even harder to make things with *him* work, whoever he was at the time. Most of all, check off the box of Sunday church, regardless. Walk in. Check the box. Walk out.

I wonder how I did what I did.

So many voices were telling me so many things. Finding *him* will make things better. The monster isn't really you . . . just keep working harder. God is watching, so go on Sundays to make him happy. I'd date guys while trying not to date girls, which was hard and confusing. I didn't want to date girls yet wanted to with everything in me. The high from being with *her*, whoever she was at the time, made the high I'd get from work approval about as potent as decaf coffee in the morning. There were moments when I thought I was crazy or on a fast track to it, because I felt so strongly about wanting a man and marriage and a family, while at the same time another part was driving me to someone and something else.

Understood

Late one night, while watching the movie *28 Days*, I finally felt as if someone understood my feelings. In the movie, Sandra Bullock plays Gwen Cummings, a successful writer who lands in rehab after ruining her sister's wedding and driving the wedding limo, drunk, through a house in a nearby neighborhood. The movie is filled with funny lines and challenging truths about life, family, and wounds. Near a turning point in the movie, Gwen's therapist is seen standing in the front of what looks like an AA meeting sharing his story. The camera flashes in as he says:

> And then I would tell myself, "Tonight I will not get wasted." And then something would happen. Or nothing would happen. And I'd get that feeling, and you all know what that feeling is: when your skin is screaming and your hands are shaking and your stomach feels like it wants to jump through your throat. And you know that if anyone had a clue how wrong it felt to be sober, they wouldn't dream of asking you to stay that way. They would say, "Oh geez, I didn't know. It's okay for you. Do that mound of cocaine. Have a drink. Have twenty drinks. Whatever you need to do to feel like a normal human being, you do it." And boy I did it. I drank and I snorted. I drank and snorted. I drank and snorted. And I did this day after day, day after day, night after night.[2]

In that moment, I felt for the first time that someone got it, got the pain of it, the pain of wanting something you weren't supposed to have. He knew my pain. He worded it perfectly. "And you know that if anyone had a clue how wrong it felt to be sober, they wouldn't dream of asking you to stay that way."

Except my pain wasn't that it felt wrong to be sober. My pain was that it felt wrong to be straight, even though that's what I wanted, but didn't, but did, but didn't. You get the battle being waged. What was supposed to be wrong felt so right.

It was the pain of that battle I'd medicate with my job. I'd also try to medicate my medicating with an hour sacrificed every Sunday in a pew hoping to appease the God whom I knew my Jekyll-and-Hyde lifestyle was offending.

I was trying to be good. After all, I wasn't gay. I was just . . . I didn't know what I was, but I was not gay, that I knew.

What I didn't know was that this hamster's wheel was about to come to a screeching halt, all at the age of twenty-six.

Undone

I was in the middle of dating someone when I must have dropped the vault, because the secrets started coming out.

For most people, when you are dating, you start by sitting next to each other. This I could do. For some couples, the next stage is snuggling on the couch, sometimes referred to as *spooning*. It was when I attempted spooning that some switch was instantly flipped in my head and produced flashes of past sexual abuse. My mind couldn't tell the difference between the images and reality. I only knew that I was trapped, which sent my body into fight-or-flight mode. As quickly as I could, I grabbed my things and left. This dreamlike moment turned into a nightmare as the memories and the images locked away in the vault all came spilling out into my conscious mind, overtaking my ability to stay in control.

Unfortunately, some of you completely understand what I am talking about. You too have had a moment when the pain from the past overtook your present and began stealing your future. You have had the nightmares in the middle of the day. You've had anxiety and fear bully you and make you step away from that relationship you most want to step toward. You've had your vault get in the way.

Have you ever tried to hug someone while holding a vault? Go find a big cardboard box, add bricks, close the lid. While holding it, try hugging someone. See how that works out for you.

Maybe that's not your story. Maybe you haven't had PTSD issues but have tried to love someone who has. You've carried the pain of the person you love the most recoiling at your safe touch. You've felt the hopelessness of sitting and waiting on the other side of the concrete wall the one you love is hiding behind. As you sit there, I wonder, what does your heart need now?

I think back to the mess of that night and the nights that would follow, the nightmares that wouldn't go away, the ones I knew had to be dealt with or another guy would be gone. This loss of control finally got me back into counseling. This time counseling was different, and this time it was for more than one session.

Counseling is only as helpful as you are open and honest and vulnerable and authentic. I don't know about you, but those are a few of my least favorite words. Vulnerable? No thank you. Open? You get hurt too easily. Authenticity wasn't my specialty either. I was too good at self-protecting, and sitting on an uncomfortable couch in front of a stranger didn't make me want to instantly unlock my vault and share all my hidden secrets. Thankfully, my new counselor was good, or maybe I was just that desperate. Either way, the vault door came open, and my counselor finally got out of me what needed to come out. I told him about the molestation when I was twenty. Unfortunately, it took too long to pry my death-like grip from this secret, and there was too much damage done to the relationship I was in. It crumbled. We broke up.

The positive of it all? Letting the secret out was freeing. My counselor suggested that a great next step might be to tell someone in my family. I grabbed all the courage I could and met with my sister one night and told her what had happened. She suggested I tell Mom.

It sounds so simple when you put it in a sentence like that: tell Mom. It was anything but simple. Telling Mom meant breaking the rules. I had to take off my protector uniform and give her the opportunity to protect me. I had to be brave enough to be weak and share that the perfect world we lived in wasn't perfect. I wasn't perfect. I was hurting. I was in need. To complicate matters, she knew the man. Who would she believe?

The terrifying day came and I told her. She fell apart as I thought she would. She called a friend as I thought she would. This is where the plot twists. She defended the man who molested me. The excuses and reasons for his choices and that season all faded into a blur of static white.

I really don't remember what happened then, except that the very, very small window of opportunity for my mom to get it right was missed. I slammed the gavel down and judged her reaction as wrong. And continued judging her, and anyone associated with her.

Especially God.

Abandoned

How do you deal with your pain? This is a moment in which I find it quite frustrating to be writing to you instead of sitting across the table from you, where we might enjoy a great cup of coffee and a warm gluten-filled, go-straight-to-your-hips-or-gut muffin or croissant. Maybe we'd sit in a couple of rockers on the back porch while drinking a cold one of whatever it is you like to drink. For me, it's sweet tea, cider beer, and Topo Chico. I am also a closet Diet Coke or Diet Dr Pepper drinker, so if I am feeling rebellious, I might share one of those with you too. A nice glass of wine also works for me from time to time. Either way, I wish I had the opportunity to hear your story.

Sometimes I get tired of my story. I get tired of my pain. Somehow, hearing someone else's story makes me feel better. It makes me feel like I am not alone in the struggle. It gives me hope when I hear how brave and tough you are. It makes me think I can be that brave too.

I wonder what your story is. What painful storms have you had to weather? How did you get through, or are you still clenching a tree in the midst of your hurricane, praying for the eye of the storm to pass over so you can have a breather? What helps you hang on?

I ask because I don't believe I handled my mom's response well at all. As I mentioned earlier, that time is gone, vanished into the oblivion of numbness and disconnection that so often accompanies something painful in one's life. This was the event that broke me. The other stuff was painful. It wounded and hurt me, to be sure, but this choice by my mother broke me.

My heart had made Mom everything, literally. She was my golden ticket. She was the one I held on to and who would be my plan B if I needed anything. Mom was supposed to be there, accident or injury, need or want. Ever since I had been a little girl without a father in my life, I had held on to my mom to make sure I wasn't alone. I had done everything to protect her so that, in some way, she might be able to take care of me.

In that moment I let my guard down and let her know my need. For once, I was choosing something that might not make her happy. I was speaking the truth about my life in the hopes of healing and happiness for me.

Her making excuses for the man who had molested me was the ultimate abandonment. It was the cliché straw that broke that camel's back. Like the little girl who left the living room so long ago with her need not met, I felt my needs didn't matter. I didn't matter. I wasn't worth protecting then; I wasn't worth protecting now.

I was done. I swore I'd never love her or talk to her again. And I was definitely done with God. I had prayed and prayed and had never felt more betrayed by him. He was the one allowing me to remain in this pain. He was the one loving and forgiving the man who had molested me and giving my mother reason to justify it. It was as if God had just forgiven the devil himself, and my mom was approving of it. If God even existed, I was done, because he had to be a coldhearted bleep-bleep if he was anything at all.

I. Was. Done.

Done trusting; done trying. I would be okay though. I wouldn't need anyone. I would make it happen on my own. I set out to do just that. Life on my own, my terms, my way, thank you very much.

Done

I was god now.

I wanted it—I bought it, medicating any insecurity with the next perfect purchase to help perfect me. I wanted it—I drank it. Since there was no God, there was no longer any need to limit anything. I could medicate any anxiety with a beverage or three. I wanted it—I dated it, and not boys. I was so done trying to make that work. Since there was no God, there were no rules and no one could disapprove of my feelings or actions. My monster had free rein. My monster loved the freedom. I could finally be free. For the first time in my life, I checked the box.

Do you know about the box? The box you check that defines your identity. There are actually multiple boxes. Glance through the ones below. Which one would you check out of each two?

☐ Male	*or*	☐	Female
☐ Introvert	*or*	☐	Extrovert
☐ Good	*or*	☐	Bad
☐ Pretty	*or*	☐	Plain
☐ Hardworking	*or*	☐	Lazy
☐ Masculine	*or*	☐	Feminine
☐ Republican	*or*	☐	Democrat
☐ Pro-choice	*or*	☐	Pro-life
☐ Smart	*or*	☐	Dumb
☐ Enough	*or*	☐	Too much
☐ Athletic	*or*	☐	Not athletic
☐ Gay	*or*	☐	Straight

For me, the box I'd struggled to know how to check ever since the monster first came out was now easily checked—gay.

A funny thing happens when you uncheck one box and check its opposite. Try it. Go through the list and think through how your life would change if you checked an opposite box. See? It changes so much, doesn't it? Which word pair brought the most change when you thought of going the other way?

For me, checking the gay box changed everything.

For starters, the monster I've been complaining about was no longer my enemy. My monster was now my friend, oh wait, not even my friend! My monster was no longer a monster! My monster was me—me the way I'd always been meant to be, right, or else why would I have battled it for so long?

Once again, I wanted it—I bought it. I bought new clothes for my new identity. Gone were the days of trying to feel like a girl. I was done trying to get the identity of the perfect woman right. After all, when I'd get one style of femininity down, they'd change it. I was done battling the fashion and image war I never felt I could get right. Here came the new me—men's cargo shorts, boys' baseball shirts, visors, ball caps. If I wasn't headed to work, this was what I was wearing. I loved it. Men didn't look at me, which made me feel safe, in control. The wardrobe helped me not to look like other women, so I didn't have to feel insecure. I didn't have to worry if I'd gotten an outfit right, because I was intentionally getting it all wrong. I could hide underneath my hat and never see the looks people were giving me.

I dated a girl, until we broke up. Then I dated someone else, until we broke up, after which I dated someone else, and so on.

Until I found someone who made me not want to date anyone else. Kristi was nice, kind, compassionate, with similar interests, and she could play golf better than anyone I'd ever met. Her parents were nice to me. They treated me like I was family, and it had been so long since I'd had any semblance of family. So she and I did it all—moved in together, got the pets, the cars, the rings, the trip to Canada, the marriage. We were the picture-perfect couple.

That was us. It was all perfect. It came with all the pleasure. There was no pain.

Isn't that the way of medicating—all the pleasure with none of the pain?

Stale Water

Unfortunately, all good drugs start to wear off at some point. But you learn to rotate them often enough to have almost a continual high. That's what I did. I rotated my drugs of choice. When work was failing, I'd lean into Kristi and she'd boost me back up. When she was down, I'd work harder, or I'd go shopping, or drink, or work out. I could go to each of these in a pinch to get the next boost to numb the pain I was unwilling to face.

Have you ever noticed this in your own medicating? That whatever you just consumed or used leaves you needing more than the time before and that there's never enough? It's a paradigm of life that has always amazed me—whatever we drink from the bottle of our choice will always leave us thirstier than before, yet we return to the bottle again and again. Believing the lie of fulfillment, we drink.

This doesn't surprise or amaze God. In fact, God warned his favorite nation, the Israelites, of this phenomenon thousands of years ago. Like us, the Israelites had a medicating problem. They kept using something to fill them, but that something wasn't God.

God chose a man named Jeremiah to be their prophet. Jeremiah had a difficult job, in that he was like the Emergency Broadcast System, speaking out God's message of warning. If you've ever had to be the bearer of bad news, you know how tough that is. Read with me one of Jeremiah's messages from God:

> But my people have changed their glory
> for that which does not profit. . . .

My people have committed two evils:
they have forsaken me,
   the fountain of living waters,
and hewed out cisterns for themselves,
   broken cisterns that can hold no water. (Jer. 2:11, 13)

Some of you, like me, may not be too big on history or farming, so you might not know what cisterns are. Back in the day, the Israelites lived in an area with very long, dry seasons and few natural springs. Due to this lack of water, they would dig cisterns, or reservoirs, underground or in rocky areas. These cisterns were used to collect and store rainwater. They would take years to dig and carve out and, if functional, would have the capacity to hold water, which could become stale.

For us Westerners who like our water cold and fresh, the idea of stagnant water might not be very appealing. And rightfully so, because it isn't, which was God's point in the passage. God was reminding them that he was the fountain of living water—always fresh, always life giving, always available. The Israelites had turned away from God and were seeking other things and people that weren't working for them. It's as if the Israelites had this beautiful fountain they walked by day after day, carrying their shovels. God points out that not only were they abandoning fresh water, but also they were not even getting stale water. No! They were going to broken cisterns incapable of holding any water! How ridiculous, right?

Aren't we just like them though? Don't we look at God, shake our heads no, grab our shovels, and walk out the door to go dig in the mud as we complain of our thirst?

Are you like me and have a broken cistern you love to go dig in? What is that broken cistern you keep going to for water? What's that job or relationship or food or drug that you dig around in, hoping it will give you life? And why do you keep going to that broken cistern, as if this time it will bring you life?

Here's the ugly truth about cisterns: they are most likely to crack in the heat when we most need the water. What happens when the thing we are depending on most for life or joy or rescue fails us?

Interesting fact: When a cistern breaks, do you know what it is used for? A tomb. That's all a broken cistern is good for.

It makes me wonder, how many people lay in a tomb they themselves dug? How many back in Jeremiah's day? How many in ours? I also wonder how it is that I'm not buried in mine. The lines and wrinkles on my face, along with the calluses on my hands from the years of hewing out one broken cistern after another, remind me I was well on my way.

5

The End of My Ways

My drive in life is from this horrible fear of being mediocre. That's always been pushing me, pushing me. Because even though I've become somebody, I still have to prove that I'm somebody. My struggle has never ended, and it probably never will.

Madonna[1]

> Why, my soul, are you downcast?
>> Why so disturbed within me?
> Put your hope in God,
>> for I will yet praise him,
>> my Savior and my God.

Psalm 42:5 NIV

How does one put into words the sadness that accompanies certain seasons of their life?

For me, 2008–9 was that season, the season of my life that I had thought, heading into it, would be filled with the most joy and fulfillment. Everything I had been working so hard to accomplish was now the way I wanted it. I finally had all my ducks in a row. I had worked my way up the coaching ladder and had just landed the big head-coaching job I'd dreamed of. I was finally going to get to call the shots and run a program *my* way.

I was also settled safely into the sixth year of my relationship with Kristi, which came with the commitment and security I had always wanted, in the gay lifestyle I had chosen as mine. We had built a house. We had dogs. We had talked about kids and maybe adopting. Her parents loved me. My golf game was even getting better.

I had arrived. I was at a point in my life where I had whatever I wanted whenever I wanted it. The only issue that was sticky to resolve inside of me was how far down into the rabbit hole I should go, you know, on the sliding feminine to masculine scale. I had slid away from the feminine side since checking the gay box because I'd never *felt* girly. I'd always felt so different from other girls, and I hated it. They made me feel vulnerable, ill-equipped, and powerless. Sliding over into the masculine world felt so freeing. Wearing boys' clothes made me feel safe and in control. Should I continue sliding even more? Should I cut my hair off? Get a gender reassignment? After all, since I felt more comfortable in guys' clothes, would going through with the other externals make my insides feel even more secure? It was a man's world, and from my vantage point, men had all the perks. Why not join them? They got to be in control and always got things their way. Many men had taught me that one.

Then I remembered something: I hated men. All they did was abuse or abandon. Why would I want to become one of them? I decided I didn't want to, which was the safer decision, because trying to be a public school teacher and pursue a gender reassignment wouldn't have gone too well. I didn't want to risk losing my job and my career. I needed the income, and I was still addicted to the approval. I did often wonder, though, if I would feel more complete as a guy, since it was so much easier to like, love, appreciate, and do guy stuff.

I settled on staying as I was and being happy with all I'd worked so hard for. I'd sit back and enjoy it all in my own little kingdom, where I got to sit on the throne. A funny thing happens when you get everything you want though. You sit on your throne, perched happily, overlooking your toy collection scattered throughout the realm you've conquered, and you realize you're *still* not happy. It wasn't until I had it all that I realized everything I had collected still left me empty. It was a horribly painful moment.

Those broken cisterns I'd built were costly. I had traded in everything to build them. Day after day I slaved away, banking on them to provide the ultimate life, but they didn't. I had thought having the gay life I'd always wanted was the one cistern I was missing to make me truly happy, but it wasn't. I was still unhappy. The pain and restlessness began seeping out of me in every way imaginable. Like any good coward, I hid behind blame.

I began to blame Kristi for my unhappiness. I convinced myself that the commitment and security of our relationship felt like a coffin. If I'd had this and that from our relationship, oh, then I'd be happy. That was it. I needed different. I needed more. I needed to be free. I told her I wasn't happy in our relationship and that it needed to change.

Oh, wait. I didn't do that. A nicer, kinder person would have, but a super coward with a propensity to protect anyone around her from pain decided that it would be too painful to tell her. Instead, I was the ultimate coward. I let my monster take a shape and form it had never taken on before, and the vilest evil came out of me. I cheated on her.

I used what I thought would make me happy. I shake my head as I type this, still not believing I did that. After all, I'd been cheated on before. I'd been left. I knew the indescribable pain it caused. Yet now I was the one causing the pain. I was a selfish coward throwing a selfish fit because the cistern I had dug wouldn't provide me with fresh water. I snuck around and did the horrible and deplorable because I thought it would make me happy.

The Bitter End

Oh, the lies we tell ourselves.

Not only did cheating not make me happy, it also left me homeless. Flash forward a couple of painful weeks later after getting caught: I am sleeping in my car in the parking lot of some random apartment complex. If you've ever wondered why some people sleep in cars, it may be because they got kicked out of their home and their community. That's what happened to me, which was good. I would have kicked me out too. I'd just ruined two people's lives with my "I want it, I get it" self-centered attitude.

My kingdom crumbled all around me. I had nowhere to go. I had no friends to call. I was in debt from my stupid "I want it, I buy it" medicating lifestyle, so I couldn't instantly fix my situation with credit cards. I lived at work and at night would drive to random parking lots and sleep in my car. I'd shower at the gym. I was miserable, but it was misery I deserved.

Thankfully, I found a benevolent person who let me rent out their guest bedroom for a few weeks. School ended with me being offered a head-coaching job in another city, so I could do what I did best—run. Summer was in full swing at this point, so I decided to get away for a week or two to Tennessee on vacation. I needed to get out of town. I needed to clear my head. I needed to figure out what the heck had gone wrong and how I'd lost control of my life.

I packed up my Tahoe and headed north along I-30, and somewhere between Dallas and the Arkansas border, driving through the Texas summer heat, it happened. I came to the end of me.

Someone Is Always to Blame

Have you ever reached the end of you? Do you know what I mean when I ask that? Maybe not, so let me explain.

I was in the sixth hour of a stretch of road that should have taken four hours to drive. I had stopped a few times—dawdled, shopped, ate—which I know sounds horrifying to you NASCAR, must-get-there-as-fast-as-you-can-type road trip people. I like to stop spontaneously and sing loudly along the way, enjoying whatever there is to enjoy. The pace of this trip had a different feel though. I needed the time in my car to sort out why I no longer had a life or friends. The questions raced: What went wrong? What had gotten me to a point so low I lost control? How could I end up so alone? Who was to blame?

I was deep in thought and reflection of the past when I was abruptly pulled to the present by a song on a CD I was listening to. One of my student athletes had made it for me. It was the second song, and as I listened to a line or two, I realized it was a Christian song. My rule for the previous eight years had been that I would never, ever listen to Christian music. After all, it was pointless, because God was an abandoning jerk and was dead to me. But as the song played, I couldn't seem to change it. Instead, I started to cry.

I quickly pulled the car over to the side of the highway and bawled. Tears streamed down my face as I stared at the reality of what my life had become, of who I had become. Everything I saw in my life I hated. A question popped into my mind: When was the last time I was happy? It was then that a memory from my backpacking days in Colorado flashed through my mind—I was standing on the side of a mountain in awe of God and feeling alive. I sat there with my hands on the steering wheel, aware that I hadn't felt anything like that since then.

In that moment, I realized something as I reflected on the destruction of my life: the greatest villain in the story of my life had been—*me*.

I was the one who had led myself to this point—my selfishness, my cowering to fear, my pride, my running, my isolation, my hiding, my blaming, my bitterness. All of it was my choice. Despite the pain from all the wounds, no one else's choice to lie to me or hurt me had been more damaging or hurtful than my choices had been. No one else had lied to me more than me. Nothing my mother, father, stepfather, or anyone else had done had hurt me as much as I had hurt myself. The trails I had traveled down were trails I chose. No one else made me walk those paths.

This realization shook me, as it was the first time I had considered that my ways couldn't be trusted. I had followed what I thought I wanted, what I thought was right, and it had turned out all wrong.

This shouldn't have been a surprise, because I had heard God's warning to the Israelites preached many times, but, in my pride and arrogance, I had written it off as not applicable to me: "The heart is deceitful above all things, and desperately sick; who can understand it?" (Jer. 17:9).

In that moment, I clearly understood my heart. I was keenly aware of how sick my heart was and that it couldn't be trusted. I glanced down the trail of the rest of my life and realized I would be destroyed if I continued on the same path. My feelings were folly. The only steps my heart would take would be toward selfish, destructive desires. It would be foolish to follow them. This was a new realization for me. As Edward Welch states, I had reached the end of me:

> We are a society of people controlled by what we think we need. It isn't until we reach the end of ourselves and realize 99 percent of our needs aren't really needs but desirous wants coming from a deceitful heart that we can even begin to make progress. Because only then will we begin to look outside of ourselves for a solution, as only then will we have reached the end of thinking and believing that we know what we need.[2]

What If

I needed something other than me, but I felt stuck. I wanted God in my life again, but didn't. The God I grew up with was angry and judgmental, and he seemed to have no ability to relate to or understand my pain. I was too tired and broken for an angry God.

Then a new question formulated in my mind: What if I was wrong? What if God was different than I thought he was?

This was a foreign concept to me. I had spent my entire life thinking God was a legalistic, angry, impatient God who was waiting for me to get it right. And even though he had sent Jesus to do his thing on the cross, God was still angry and would rather judge me than save me. When I couldn't get my life right, I tried closing my eyes and pretending he didn't exist.

But what if both were wrong? What if he was there and was actually good? What if he knew I was incapable of doing anything good? What if—dare I say it?—what if he actually cared about me? Not only the world, or orphans, or starving children. What if he cared about *me*?

On the side of I-30 that day, I said, "God, if you are out there and are really God, you have to be better than I think you are. I am going to give you a year, one year, and I will do whatever you ask. I am not going to put you in any kind of a box. I just want to find out if you are different than I think you are and if you actually do care about me." If my search for God led me to a temple or a mosque or somewhere else, I'd roll with it. I'd never understood the small Christian box. I figured if Jesus really was God and was better than I thought he was, he could handle me allowing him to appear in whatever form he wanted.

So . . . I opened the box.

The Beggar in Me

I put the car back into drive and headed on to Tennessee, beginning the first hour of my 365-day experiment with God. I figured I had to do only two things: simply look and listen for God everywhere. It was kind of exciting. Like a child constantly glancing out the window on Christmas Eve looking for Santa, I drove looking out the window, waiting to see if God would show up.

I pause here to ask: Have you ever tried it? Have you ever invited God to show up in your life? He promises in Scripture that he will:

You will seek me and find me when you seek me with all your heart. (Jer. 29:13 NIV)

> I love those who love me,
> and those who seek me diligently find me. (Prov. 8:17)

Draw near to God, and he will draw near to you. (James 4:8)

> You came near when I called on you;
> you said, "Do not fear!" (Lam. 3:57)

He says he will show up, but did you notice something? He is willing to reveal himself when what you really want is him. Notice the diligent seeking with all your heart, and notice what you are seeking—him, not things, not what he can do for you. When you want *him*, then he will reveal himself. It's about wanting him with all your heart.

For me, if I am honest, I'd lived as though Scripture said:

You will seek gifts and find toys, when you seek them with all your heart. (JustgivemewhatIwant 29:13)

I love those who work, and those who seek me diligently find promotions. (Probably 8:17)

Draw near to God, and he will give you a better future. (Hallucinations 4:8)

You came near when I called on you; you said, "Go shopping!" (Laments 3:57)

That's how I had really sought him. I had asked Jesus to save me at the age of thirteen and then had spent a lifetime treating him like a temperamental vending machine, which required you to put the coins in "just so" while hitting the buttons "just right." If you did, voilà! Out would pop the reward of your choice. He was an eternal Santa Claus, and if I stayed on the good list, then at least once a year he would travel down from the north pole of heaven and give me good things. I wanted his things for my kingdom. I wanted him on my terms, for my way.

Now, with my kingdom lying around me in rubble, I was tired of the emptiness that accompanied things and relationships. I was a beggar, sitting on a pile of emptiness and disappointments, waiting and begging for God to show up. He did.

Before he swoops into the story and saves the day, let me answer one question I often hear. I heard it when I used the term *beggar* three sentences up. Some of you are wondering why God seems so narcissistic, waiting until we beg like a dog before he shows up. Let me say first that God is not narcissistic. If he was anything other than love, he couldn't have sent his Son, Jesus, to die on the cross. A true narcissist can't sacrifice for others, as he or she is too selfish.

Does God want me to be a beggar? Maybe it's not a question to answer but a reality to face. It's not that God wants me to be a beggar but that he wants me to be aware that I am a beggar. In fact, Jesus sees this as so important that it is the first thing he says in an early public appearance. Picture a mountainside, possibly on a sunny day. Jesus is sitting. A large crowd gathers around him. As any great orator knows, the first words out of your mouth are the most important, so the first sentence out of his mouth is "Blessed are the poor in spirit, for theirs is the kingdom of heaven" (Matt. 5:3 NIV).

Ta-da! You're moved, aren't you? I know. That's one powerful opening statement, Jesus. Of all the ways, the trails, and the journeys I have traveled, there was only one worth traveling, the way of hope, which begins here. In these thirteen words, one can begin to be blessed, and blessed is just a fancy word for happy. If you continue to read Matthew 5, the first eight statements Jesus makes will give you a road map to a happy life, which makes these first thirteen words so very important. I know you too want to live a happy life.

I pause here to notice what he didn't say, what I might have put first:

Blessed are those who have a lot of money, for they will never need.

Blessed are those who are straight and have great marriages, for they will never feel alone.

Blessed are those who are gay and can legally wed, for they will be happy.

Blessed are those who parent well, for they will be blessed by their kids.

Blessed are those who are famous, for they will be remembered forever.

No. Jesus says none of that. Notice instead whom he begins with: the poor in spirit. Most people read this and think of those who don't make much money. To fully understand what Jesus means, we need to take a look at the Greek, the original language in which the New Testament was written.

There are multiple words for *poor* in the Greek used in Scripture. One such word is *penace*, as in she was so poor she had to work for food. However, the Greek word Jesus uses here is *ptōchos*, which means beggar—as in helpless, powerless to accomplish an end. *Penace* poor can work, can earn, can make something happen. *Ptōchos* poor cannot. They are so destitute they can't do or earn a thing to make their lives better.

Glance over these two Greek terms again:

penace: earn   *ptōchos*: beg

What are your thoughts as you look at them? Me too. I'd much rather earn than beg. That's what I'd been trying to do—earn my happiness, earn my security, earn my worth.

But Jesus uses the word *ptōchos* and says that's where the blessings begin. Jesus opens his ministry in front of the whole world and says blessed are those who know they are beggars. Blessed are those who know they are powerless to do anything or accomplish anything on their own. I like how John Baker describes it: "I admit that I am powerless to control my tendency to do the wrong thing and that my life is unmanageable."[3]

Isn't that a kick in the pants? Despite my best efforts—my scheduling, my doing, my striving—my life is still and always will be unmanageable. I want to try to manage it, don't I? I want to control it, earn it. But listen as Jesus whispers, "Don't."

This is kind of a tough statement to swallow, Jesus, especially for us Americans, right? We don't beg. We work hard. We earn. We pull ourselves up by our bootstraps. At least that's what we do in Texas. We work hard to be independent and self-sufficient.

In Jesus's opening statement, he shatters our do-it-yourself American way. It needs shattering, because we can't do it ourselves. We just don't want to admit it. I sure didn't. But freedom begins when you are able to finally admit that you are living in a prison cell. My prison cell was my inability, my absolute powerlessness to make anything happen in my life. I can't even control when I take my next breath. If I can't control that one simple yet necessary requirement for my existence, then who am I to think I can control anything else? Freedom comes when I know and feel the truth of my poverty. John Piper states, "When Jesus says, 'Blessed are the poor in spirit,' He does not mean everybody. He means those who feel it."[4]

In my Tahoe that day, I felt my poverty. I knew it. I knew how powerless I really was to do anything right or to accomplish anything good in my life. I knew how dark my heart was when left alone to guide me. I knew that I had built my kingdom in an effort to hide this truth from everyone, including me. I was powerless to protect anything or anyone, much less myself.

What becomes available in that moment of powerlessness is the ability to have access to true power. As David Benner says,

"Self-acceptance always precedes genuine self-surrender and self-transformation."[5] Transformation began as I uncrossed my arms and opened the posture of my heart toward God, which was only possible as I opened my eyes to the reality of myself.

The Designer's Touch

Some of you don't buy this truth still. I know. It's tough to swallow, because you are you. You are a hard worker. You are the one using those gifts and talents to earn that paycheck. You are out there in the world, making it happen. You're right. You are doing all of that.

But let me ask you, Who gave you those gifts and talents? Where did they come from? Who gave you the ability to get up this morning, to move your body throughout the day, to continue breathing as you read this? Where does all of this come from? Who created you?

King David answers these questions in Psalm 139:

> For you created my inmost being;
>> you knit me together in my mother's womb.
> I praise you because I am fearfully and wonderfully made;
>> your works are wonderful,
>> I know that full well.
> My frame was not hidden from you
>> when I was made in the secret place,
>> when I was woven together in the depths of the earth.
> Your eyes saw my unformed body;
>> all the days ordained for me were written in your book
>> before one of them came to be. (vv. 13–16 NIV)

Do you see God creating you, picking out your unique talents, gifts, and traits? Do you see him knowing the exact number of breaths you will take? Do you see that power?

It is a different kind of power than what I have. He knows the exact number of breaths I will take. *Me?* I don't even know when I am going to sneeze sometimes.

As for that ability to work hard and earn those gifts, James says, "Every good and perfect gift is from above, coming down from the Father of the heavenly lights, who does not change like shifting shadows" (James 1:17 NIV). God reminds us where the real power comes from. Not to be Debbie Downer here, but even the most powerful of us has yet to figure out a way to overcome old age and death. Death is the ultimate reminder, isn't it? But it doesn't have to be something we fear, as God tells us in Isaiah 46:

> Even to your old age and gray hairs
> I am he, I am he who will sustain you.
> I have made you and I will carry you;
> I will sustain you and I will rescue you. (v. 4 NIV)

This life is hard, and we are all keenly aware of our fragility, our powerlessness, our need of sustenance. Even the amazingly talented Madonna feels her inadequacy when she says, "My struggle has never ended, and it probably never will." If the popular and talented Madonna feels inadequate, how can we mere unknown mortals stand a chance? We don't.

We are left with only two options. Fight for all the power we can get, as the world teaches. Or hear Jesus's words spoken from the side of the mountain and acknowledge the reality of our hearts.

Humbly admit your powerlessness and invite Jesus, the provision of power and purpose, into your life. Stop trying. Stop controlling. Stop isolating yourself, because here's the truth: the greatest enemy to living an empowered life is self-sufficiency. Jesus invites you to strip off the fake clothes and sit atop your pile of rubble, as I did that day, and wait for him to come near to you, as he did to me.

I made it to Tennessee that night, and to my surprise, on the nightstand of the guest room where I was staying, I found a Bible. That night, before turning off the light, I picked up that old blue Bible (half expecting lightning to strike, since I hadn't picked one up in eight years) and started reading. I have no idea what I read that night. What I do know is that something different happened. The words jumped off the page as I read them. I understood them and felt them in a way I had never experienced before. In all those Sundays of sitting in a church pew, or in the five semesters of Bible classes I took in college, or the countless times I previously read Scripture on my own, I had never experienced what I did that night. I knew . . . *he had heard me! God had shown up!*

This was great for a day or two until reality and terror hit me, when I realized that God wanted me to go back to church.

6

The Way of Hope

> When I'm on stage, I'm trying to do one thing: bring people joy.
> Just like church does. People don't go to church to find trouble;
> they go there to lose it.
>
> James Brown[1]

I turned forty this year. Middle age sounds like a bad disease.
A few friends of mine joked that they were going on a cruise
for a month around my birthday, so they wouldn't have to deal with
me while I faced the reality of this turning point. I believe I actually have handled turning forty pretty well, thank you very much.
Turning thirty-nine made me kind of lose it for a week or two.
However, forty has been a little better, and I find with its arrival I
am noticing more profoundly the upside and downside of aging.

On the one hand, I am saddened by the way my body reacts or
responds—or doesn't. Why does your bladder have to speed up
while your metabolism slows down? Why can't that be reversed?
Why can't I walk silently into the kitchen for a cup of coffee in
the morning without waking up everyone in the house with the

sounds of my joints popping and creaking? I know this is just the beginning. Growing older isn't for wimps.

On the other hand, there is an upside to aging. While my body may not work as well, I think my brain is faring better. I find that being older has also brought wisdom. And how priceless is wisdom? If you spend any time in Scripture, you will quickly see that God is a big fan of it, so much so that wisdom is mentioned in 201 verses. Here are three of my favorites:

> The fear of the LORD is the beginning of knowledge,
>   but fools despise wisdom and instruction.
>   (Prov. 1:7 NIV).

> Listen to advice and accept discipline,
>   and at the end you will be counted among the wise.
>   (Prov. 19:20 NIV)

If any of you lacks wisdom, you should ask God, who gives generously to all without finding fault, and it will be given to you. (James 1:5 NIV)

Those are great nuggets of wisdom on wisdom, eh? May I share one more? It's not nearly as important, and it doesn't come from the Bible. But I find this piece of wisdom very helpful.

There are two kinds of people in this world. It's very important to learn the difference between them and to know which kind you are. The two kinds of people? Those who camp and those who do not.

Yes, friend. There are two distinct types of people, and a wise person knows the difference and never tries to vacation with the other. Let me clarify . . . when I say camp, I mean camp. Some of you read that and instantly think pop-up or RV. No, no, no. I am sorry to break it to you, but that's not camping. I hear some of you arguing with me that it is camping, because you're not at home and you're spending the night "in nature," but you're not really in nature. You're in a safer and often bigger and better-built housing structure than most people in third-world countries live in, and you have electricity and running water.

According to the MF dictionary (mine), camping is defined as a recreational outdoor activity in which at least one night is spent in a temporary structure made of four bearing poles not to exceed half an inch in diameter and that does not have wheels. The only electricity allowed on such an outing is the electricity found during a sunrise, sunset, or passionate kiss, and the only running water allowed is that of fresh water in a nearby stream or river. An outing in that type of environment is camping. Yes, I admit it: I am a camping nerd.

I understand this puts me in a small segment of society, as most people are non-campers who prefer cushions, comfort, electricity, and bathrooms. I prefer to risk rooming with creepy crawlies and not complain when I wake up sore (from a rock I accidently slept on) in order to gain the purity of the unexplored and uninhabited. My body doesn't mind paying the price in order for me to have a front-row seat to view an expanse of sky where shining celestial stars are the skyline, free from the marring of skyscrapers.

Mostly I love camping because I get to sit by a fire and watch the embers burn. I enjoy listening to the crackle of a fire accompanied by the symphonic sound of nature's nighttime orchestra. The right fire can melt the chill off any night and can illuminate the best conversations. A fire brings life.

I am not a pyromaniac, but I love to start fires. I love how they begin with smoke and then that first little cinder ignites a flame. Then it spreads, sometimes slowly, painfully, requiring attention and encouragement from an added twig, kindling, or soft breeze. At other times, the conditions are so perfect that the little ember bursts into what seems like an instantaneous roaring flame. Its birth is beautiful to me. My life has resembled such a fire.

Testing, Testing

The ending of my ways brought respite from the storms of my life. As the rain subsided, the glow of an embryonic ember could be seen—one that the Holy Spirit had ignited so long ago. I felt the little ember of hope flickering in my soul, and I became eager to see it grow. But the nudge of the next step had me paralyzed.

I heard it. I knew it, but no magical metaphor could describe the fear I felt in doing it. I was petrified of going back to church.

Mile after mile of my trip back to Texas was filled with my searching for excuses to appease God's request. I was in a pickle. Days before I had made my blanket declaration that I would do whatever he asked. I knew he was asking me to do this. I hated it.

I thought I had found a new way to travel, *The Way of Hope*. I didn't fully know or understand it, but I knew if there was a new way to travel through life, it had to be with God. I had to travel with him and see him in a way I'd never pictured or imagined him before. I didn't want a church full of people throwing a wet blanket on the growing flame inside my soul. I was wounded. I was scared to death of crawling to church only to be kicked by some self-righteous "saint" standing proudly guarding the door. Could I find a church where the person I met at the door was humble enough to know he or she was a beggar too?

I didn't want to be wounded again by church. I knew the script of the sermons. I had "walked the walk" and "talked the talk" once before. I had once been the self-righteous "saint" standing at the door. I knew what I would have thought if someone as broken as me had walked up to it. But since I was open to my view of God being wrong, what if my view of church was wrong too? What if there was a church I could find that might help shed light on this way of hope?

I set out to do the impossible—find a church for people like me. I felt as though there were only two doors I could walk through. Churches usually fall into two categories when it comes to the same-sex lifestyle: the way of condemning or the way of condoning.

I didn't want to walk through the door of either type of church. I didn't want a church that condemned me for who I was or what I had done. I already had enough voices of self-condemnation and shame in my head to fill every seat or pew. I knew I was far from being a saint, and I didn't need to be reminded or have a door slammed in my face for being a sinner. I didn't need anyone else to tell me my life, as of late, had been wrong. I hadn't at that point made the decision to leave the lifestyle. I wasn't even thinking about my sexuality at that time. I was just trying to figure out God and see if he really was good.

I also didn't need church to be hyper-focused on my sexuality because, for once in my life, I wasn't, which is why I didn't want to walk through the door of a church that condoned the same-sex lifestyle either. I didn't want to go to a church that celebrated it. Why would I want to go to a church that condoned something I hated. Yes, you can be gay and hate it. Granted, there are those who say they celebrate it and love it, but there are some who hate the struggle, the attraction, and wish they were straight.

You see, it can be a really hard life being gay. You always feel different because you are. You are in the minority, and you are reminded of it every day. Even as the same-sex lifestyle is normalized in society, I hypothesize that at some core level it is never normalized inside your soul. Even when I was a proud LGBT member, I hated it but didn't want to let anyone, especially myself, know it. Like a rookie at the high rollers' table for the first time, I'd taken everything and bet it on one hand: that being gay would make me happy. I had pushed all my chips in for red-14, and when the roulette wheel began to slow down, I knew I was screwed. The ball didn't land where I thought it would. Living that life didn't make me any happier or bring me any more peace than I'd had before. I couldn't let anyone know that though, most of all myself. I'd either lie to myself or blame it on the person I was with in order to avoid acknowledging that something might be wrong or off inside of me.

So I set off on the impossible task of finding a church that didn't condone or condemn but might offer something different. Maybe I could find a church that could just offer space. Maybe I could find a place where I could sit silently and absorb God on a Sunday morning. I braved Google and searched online for a church that might be close to what I was looking for. I had no clue what kind of a church I really needed or even wanted. I only knew what I didn't want.

Let'SEXpress

I found what appeared to be a safe option that next Sunday. It was a small Bible church that was new. I pulled into the parking lot ten minutes before the service started, and I walked into the building ten minutes late. During those sweat- and fear-filled twenty minutes, I sat in my car like a private detective, watching every person who walked into the building, judging how mean or nice each looked, internally pointing at every hypocrite who walked by, trying to find an excuse not to walk in the door. I wanted to find some self-righteous person who could justify my list of excuses to present to God for not going in. I did finally go in. I don't remember much about the service, other than leaving early and thinking I couldn't go there because it met in a school cafeteria. I was a teacher, and I didn't want to be in a school on Sunday.

The next Sunday I went through the same routine. Ten minutes before the service started, I pulled into the parking lot of a nearby megachurch. It felt fake and plastic, and I remember wondering if the pastor onstage had more makeup on than I did. Then I remembered I didn't wear makeup that day. I once again left early, knowing that all of their upright perfect posture could never understand my crawling on the floor.

I spent the next few days feeling defeated and wanting to burn whatever haystack that needle was hidden in, because that's how my search for a church felt. Luckily, I had started my new job that week, which was exciting. It was the week before school started, which for teachers is filled with riveting staff development meetings that thoroughly prepare you for the year ahead of herding cats.

I was driving to a nearby high school for that day's staff meeting and was about a mile from it when I noticed a weird-shaped, orange building on my left. I read the sign and realized it was a church. My eyes darted to the banner waving in the grass just past the sign. It was a black banner that read, "Let'SEXpress," and below that were the various messages in the Sunday series. The last message in the series: Same Sex.

I instantly started perspiring as I wondered what Gateway Church was about and what they would be saying the Sunday morning of that last message, which just happened to be the following week. The instant nausea and early onset hot flash I felt registered in my soul as a nudge that I was supposed to go. Ugh.

That night I went on the church's website to learn what they were all about. What I read there were four words that were catalytic in changing my life and propelling me forward down the way of hope. The words? Come as you are.

Come as You Are

These words excited, perplexed, and frightened me all at the same time. What if they were really true? Was this a church that was welcoming me to come as I really was? A hot mess? Could I come without cleaning up, fixing up, or brushing up on my Christianese? What if there really was a place I could crawl into with my wounded soul?

And yet I was perplexed. How could they let me come just as I was? Didn't I need to "get it all together"? How quickly would they expect me to "clean up"? I knew the train wreck that lay inside my soul. God had given me a glimpse of it on that I-30 "road to Damascus" experience, and I knew it wouldn't be a four-weeks-and-you're-done thing. I wanted to be healed. I didn't want to just change a behavior or two. I had tried behavior management churches. I didn't need more decades of that. I was scared, scared that they meant "come as you are" with a hidden, invisible parenthesis that read (unless you are gay), because every church has a line you can't cross (in order to be in the club). Or you must cross the line in a certain time frame, depending on the thing. You get the point.

I combed through the rest of the website looking for what was wrong with them. Isn't it funny the self-defeating games we play? Hiding behind judgments? You do it too; admit it. You judge to stay safe. You judge and reject others before they can reject you. We all do it.

As I looked through the rest of the website, it seemed safe and normal for a church claiming to like Jesus. (That's the other funny thing, isn't it? Actually, it's not funny but tragically sad, the way churches or church people say they like Jesus and then do things in his name that he would never do.) I didn't see any of that on the website, so I took it one step further and I listened to a sermon podcast from a previous week. I laughed while listening to it, which felt good and yet a little odd, because it was a church sermon. Who laughs at those? Is that even allowed?

The laughter quickly turned to tears, because whatever he was saying, which I can't recall now, hit me in the middle of my soul. Square peg, square hole. What he was saying nailed me. I laughed again. Then I cried again, then laughed more. This cycle continued, because I immediately listened to another sermon podcast after the first one ended. Then I listened to another, and another.

It was about 1:00 a.m. when I did something I still can't believe I did. I searched back through the website and found the lead pastor's name—some guy named John Burke—and I emailed him. I told this complete stranger that I was coming to his church that next Sunday, that I had been in the lifestyle, that he had better not say it was wrong, that he had better not say it was right, that I didn't know what I wanted him to say but that he had better say something because I was coming. I was hurting. This felt like my last hope.

As tears streamed down my face, I hit send, closed my laptop, and cried myself to sleep. I went about the next day going to meetings, weirdly counting down the hours until the day ended, which would put me one day closer to Sunday. I got home that night, opened my computer, and to my horrific surprise saw an email that made me literally jump back from my laptop. The name of the sender? John Burke. He had emailed me back.

I froze. Do I open it? What will it say? An internal silent scream emitted from my body in all directions. With a scared, shaking, please-don't-make-me-do-it pointer finger, I opened it and read it.

The words were nice. He said he was excited for me to come on Sunday. He invited me to come down front to meet him after the service was over. He was praying for me.

I closed the email and went in the bathroom and threw up. Not really. I didn't throw up, but I probably could have. I somehow felt seen by God again. This pastor sounded so real, but then again, it was an email. It could have been written by an assistant or some lackey. I would have to go on Sunday to see if he was real.

Sunday

Sunday came. I pulled into the parking lot fifteen minutes early. I scouted out the enemies in the parking lot for only five minutes this time. I had decided to go in early so I could have a strategic seat close to the door if things got ugly—center back, floor section, third row from the back, aisle seat. That girl with the hat pulled down low, hiding—that was me.

I sat frozen as the enemies walked in, filling the seats around me. Finally, the lights dropped lower and the band started playing worship songs. I sat frozen, fighting tears and nausea. Announcements came and went, and I assumed that John Burke would be stepping onstage to speak. I didn't expect what happened next instead: a video played depicting "Christian" gay haters holding signs and picketing. The song made it clear this video was showing the travesty associated with this kind of behavior. The video wasn't on hating gays but on "Christian" gay haters. The video ended and John came onstage, adjusted his music stand podium, and opened with an apology. A preacher was apologizing to the gay community. I couldn't believe it.

That was only the beginning. John spoke humbly from his own story and his own struggle with gay people. He shared how he felt God calling him to pastor a church that was called to love the lost and the broken—the dechurched, unchurched, and disenfranchised. In that confusing list of titles, he knew this meant he was called to love those in the same-sex lifestyle. Despite his fears, despite his feelings, he admitted truth. He didn't know anyone gay, much less know how to love them.

As John continued to speak, I felt hope rising. I felt seen and understood, and then it got even better. Three brave people, whom I now call my heroes of the faith, were called up on the stage. For the next twenty or so minutes, they shared the stories of healing and redemption they had experienced in this "come as you are" faith community.

I couldn't believe it! People from the same-sex lifestyle were talking on the stage of a church about being gay, about their struggles, about being loved by church people, about God being safe and good! They shared about surrendering, healing, and their continued struggles. They talked about both not condoning their struggle and not being condemned for it! As I listened to these three individuals share about their journeys, the tiny ember in my soul felt the winds of their testimony, and as when fresh pieces of dry wood are added to a fire, the flame roared anew. Their courageous stories ignited hope in me, and once again, I knew God had seen me. He had heard me. He was leading me one step further down the way of hope.

I think about the power of the stories shared that day and wonder, what's your story? Are you a hero of the faith in whom

God has moved mountains and worked miracles? Have you shared your story lately, regardless of how big or small those mountains or miracles may have been? I believe it's something that our text-it-or-tweet-it, one-hundred-and-forty-characters-maximum-please culture doesn't slow down enough for. When we don't slow down enough to share our stories, Satan wins, because there is power in our stories—so much so that Satan is scared of them.

The apostle John shared: "And they have conquered him by the blood of the Lamb and by the word of their testimony, for they loved not their lives even unto death" (Rev. 12:11). Did you see that? The one-two punch knockout of Satan happens by Jesus's blood and by our stories. Satan can't one-up the power of Jesus working in our lives and our talking about it! So I wonder, who do you need to tell your story to? What has God been up to in your life lately that could inspire others to hope for more in their own? What do you need to do to slow down your life enough to have time to share a meal and your story? It is not the blood of the Lamb and a really great sermon that kicks Satan's tail. It's not Jesus plus a great Five Steps to Healing book. No, it's the blood of the Lamb and our stories that bring victory over the enemy. Your story matters.

Maybe you are new to this whole God thing and are trying to decide if there really is a Satan. Is he really evil and an enemy? Oh yes. He is real. He is evil. His whole desire, since you were born, has been to destroy you and to take away as much love and happiness from your life as he can. Listen to the contrast between his desire for your life and Jesus's desire: "The thief comes only to steal and kill and destroy. I came that they may have life and have it abundantly" (John 10:10).

Satan comes to destroy your life. Jesus comes to give you an abundant one. Maybe your life has been filled with more destruction than abundance. Maybe you are in need of hope. Maybe you need to hear that your struggle, whatever it is, can be overcome.

To you I say, hang in there and listen with me. Listen to those four words that moved my heart all those years ago.

Come. As. You. Are.

These are not the words of either Gateway or John Burke. They are words spoken by Jesus to you: "Come to me, all you who are weary and burdened, and I will give you rest" (Matt. 11:28 NIV).

Reread it, please. Notice what Jesus doesn't say. He doesn't say, "Come to me, all you who have it all together, and I will celebrate you then," or "Come to me, all you who have quit that habitual sin, and I will help you with the rest," or "Come to me, all you who have no doubts about me, and then I will love you." No, Jesus doesn't say any of that. He simply says come. Tired, weary, broken, or burdened, come.

Here's the question: What's stopping you? What's stopping you from coming to Jesus just as you are? Not the cleaned-up, picked-up, got-it-all-together you, but the real you, the messy, can't-make-it-any-better, I-know-because-I've-tried you. Why not have a conversation with him today about the mess of your life covering the masterpiece underneath?

Is it pride or fear? If you're like me, it's usually both. Let's speak to the fear. What are you afraid of? That he will be angry? He will reject you? He will be harsh and mean and make you do things you don't want to do? Listen to Jesus's reply to those questions: "Come to me, all you who are weary and burdened, and I will give you rest. Take my yoke upon you and learn from me, for I am gentle and humble in heart, and you will find rest for your souls. For my yoke is easy and my burden is light" (Matt. 11:28–30 NIV).

What did you hear there? How did that stand up to those fears? Let's tackle the fear of rejection head-on, as I know it's a big one; after all, you know what you've done. You know how messy your life has been. You know the affair you committed, the bottle you can't put down, or the judgmental words you can't stop speaking. You know you. You struggle with accepting you, so why would he? It's simple. He's not you.

He knows what you've been doing. He knows why you've been doing it. More importantly though, he knows what you were created for. He sees what is and what could be. You both know you can leave your ways of doing life. You both know those ways aren't working for you. Today can be different as you begin walking the way of hope as well. Four simple words invite you. They've changed a little though, as he wants to help with the fear of rejection you are battling. His words: Come to me, all.

You see that? It says all, which in the Greek happens to mean all. All includes you—you the adulterer, you the lesbian, you the liar, you the abused and ashamed, you the one who likes to cheat on your taxes, you the one who can't control your eating, you the porn addict. You.

All means all. All means you are invited too.

For those still doubting, I hate to inform you, but your sin is not so special that what Jesus did on the cross didn't cover it. It did. It's covered and forgiven with only one question to be answered: Do you want what Jesus accomplished on the cross to count for you?

Jesus is inviting you to come. Will you? As you are?

Do you feel the tug of pride and ego pull you back? Do you feel the tension between the simple invitation to come but notice that, in doing so, you'd have to leave where you are? It's a kicker, I know. To come means you have to go. You have to leave where you are in your life, which is usually a place of comfort where you are in control. Pride usually has you at your red "you are here" dot for a reason. There is something that pride and ego get from you being right there, wherever you are in your life. Pride and ego like being there, because you get to be in control. Staying where you are lets you be god. Jesus simply nods in acknowledgment of where you are and whispers, "Come as you are and let me be God." Our pride never likes that. Pride never wants to leave. Pride doesn't want to learn a new way, because learning is work. Learning requires some doing. Pride is a lazy old dog that doesn't want to learn any new tricks.

Let's not jump ahead of ourselves to the doing yet. Let's linger at *being* some more, because that's the beautiful thing—to just be.

Noisy or Restful

Most of us aren't good at being, but it's what we were created as—human beings, whose job is to be with God. That was our original created design, the one we see in the garden. With these four words, come as you are, Jesus invites us back to creation. Jesus invites us to simply come and be. Charles Spurgeon's words from 1871 express this truth so beautifully:

> If you want rest, O weary souls, ye can find it nowhere until ye come and lay your burdens down at his dear pierced feet, and find life in looking alone to Him. Come ye needy, come and welcome; come and take the rest ye need. Jesus saith to you, "Come and take what I freely give." Without money come, without merit come, without preparation come. It is just, come, come now; come as you are, come with your burden, come with your yoke, though the yoke be the yoke of the devil, and the burden be the burden of sin, yet come as you are, and the promise shall be fulfilled to you, "I will give you rest."[2]

It's a simple invitation—to come and be. Come and rest. I like it. I need it. Do you?

This leads me to another question: If Jesus invites all to come, shouldn't we? For you church folks reading this who do the church thing, shouldn't our invitation be for all? Come, all you who are crawling. Crawl on in. What if church was the one place where the messy and messed up could come crawling in to find rest? Isn't that what it is supposed to be?

Pauline Phillips, the original Dear Abby columnist, wrote, "A church is a hospital for sinners, not a museum for saints."[3] If so, why do we so often find churches that don't act like a hospital? How tragic would it be to see a hospital turn a patient away because he was sick or bleeding? It wouldn't be a hospital! What if we, the church, could truly be a hospital where wounded hearts could come to find healing? Think about it. What would that look like? What would people experience? What would they see? What would they hear?

I know one thing they wouldn't hear. A gong. Are you familiar with a gong? Have you heard one? Imagine with me, if you will, the most annoying sound you can think of. Seriously, take a moment. Imagine it. How annoying was it? Was it as annoying as nails on a chalkboard or car alarms going off at 3:00 a.m.? Maybe it was as annoying as your spouse's snoring or a dial-up modem.

Well, that's what Paul says the church sounds like when we don't love. When wounded people aren't allowed to come as they are, they hear the gong and feel its reverberation. Listen to Paul's words:

> If I speak in the tongues of men and of angels, but have not love, I am a noisy gong or a clanging cymbal. And if I have prophetic powers, and understand all mysteries and all knowledge, and if I have all faith, so as to remove mountains, but have not love, I am nothing. If I give away all I have, and if I deliver up my body to be burned, but have not love, I gain nothing. (1 Cor. 13:1–3)

This is a challenging passage for me and maybe for you as well. I can be spiritually gifted, theologically equipped, and sacrificial to the point of death, but if I don't love in the process, I am as annoying as a 1998 dial-up modem (and about as effective too).

Closed for Business

Paul reminds us of what love really is:

> Love is patient and kind; love does not envy or boast; it is not arrogant or rude. It does not insist on its own way; it is not irritable or resentful; it does not rejoice at wrongdoing, but rejoices with the truth. Love bears all things, believes all things, hopes all things, endures all things. (1 Cor. 13:4–7)

We hear Jesus whisper, "Come as you are. Let me love you."

For you church people, does your church whisper it too? Does your small group, life group, home group, missionally minded/ Beth Moore studying/men's/women's/whatever the flavor of your group whisper it too? I ask that here because this is who Paul is speaking to: the church in Corinth, the church today. After spending hours teaching, rebuking, cheering, and reminding the Corinthians, he exhorts them with sixteen simple verses to do what is most important: love.

It's love that drew a sinner like me onto the way of hope. It's love that keeps me walking on it and continues to lead me. On the way of hope, love allows me to come as I am, at any point in the journey, and find love. The way of hope is a way of welcoming grace, whispering, "Let me love you." I wonder, does your life whisper it too?

Does it shout it out to the tattooed, different-from-you culture around you, to the sinner still swimming in his sin, to the abused and abandoned, the uptight and arrogant, the pretty and popular, the male and the masculine, the sexually broken, disoriented, or disqualified?

Like a blinking neon sign that loudly welcomes all to enter in, does your life naturally welcome others? Who, when you come near them, see them, or pass them, does the sign instantly shut off for and switch to Closed for Business?

We all have them, don't we? The people we'd rather not do life with. We (naturally) let other people love on them. They are messy. They are difficult. They are _____ (fill in whatever you know belongs here), followed by the ever-popular excuse, "I just don't connect with them."

Jesus whispers again, "Love your neighbor."

You think you do. You love the people around you. But have you noticed something? Take a look at who's around you. Doesn't it naturally happen that you end up in a job with people "like you," in a housing area with people "like you," and at a church with people "like you"?

Take this litmus test: think of the closest twelve people in your life or the last twelve people you have invited into your home, not counting family members, cleaning ladies, or repairmen. How different are they from you? Are they of another race, another tax bracket, another sex or sexual preference, another religion?

What about your church? How's the diversity there?

When Jesus was asked by a lawyer (who wanted some attaboys) about this "come as you are, who is my neighbor, and do I really have to love them" concept, Jesus told a parable of a man robbed, beaten, and left for dead (see Luke 10). A priest and a Levite each walked by, both men of purpose and position, in the public eye, whose positions should have bent them toward kindness, compassion, and charitable acts. But both men stepped aside and walked on. The one who stopped? The Samaritan. The outcast, not-good-enough, don't-invite-them-inside-type person. He stopped and rendered aid and showed love to this hurting soul. As the gong echoed, the religious and elite just walked on by.

Pastors or small group leaders, if you want your church, group, or community to help the hurting, you have to do it too—not preach it, not teach it, but actually be the one to walk alongside and love. If you haven't had a gay man, woman, or couple in your home, don't expect your church or group to. As the leader goes, so goes the group. If you love those different from you, those around you will too.

I shudder to think of where my life would be if John Burke hadn't been willing to work through his fears, decades ago, so that years later I would have a place to work through mine. It was the open door of a "come as you are" church that served as the IV I needed to give my soul the necessary nutrients I lacked.

We need more hospitals—not museums.

Home

The place God created for the hurting to find hope is the church. The church was designed to be a hospital, a refuge, a home. Don't we all want a place to call home—a place where we can be known and still loved, where we can be loved even when we aren't lovely? We all need it and desire it, so turn the page as we dive further into this need, because the way of hope requires us to walk *The Way of Community.*

7

The Way of Community

You can run away from yourself so often, and so much, just because
the broken pieces of you cut your feet too deeply if you stay around
for too long. But then what if someone were to come along and pick
up those pieces for you? Then you wouldn't have to run away from
yourself anymore. You could stop running. If someone sees you as
something worth staying with—maybe you'll stay with yourself too.

C. JoyBell C. [1]

Moving truths such as "God loves me" from our heads to our
hearts is often difficult. It is possible, but only as we journey with
others. The God who is divine community is known only in human
community. Deep knowing of perfect love, just like deep knowing of ourselves, demands that we be in relationships of spiritual
friendship. No one should ever expect to make the journey alone.

David Benner [2]

I liked the church.
They had coffee, animal crackers, relevant teaching, and
an atmosphere that felt real. I could slip in and slip out and then

breathe. It was a nice little rhythm. Sadly, it was only a couple of weeks before the high of my new job and the new church wore off.

Then I felt the pain of loneliness.

Do you know this pain? I believe it's one of the most painful pains out there. As you may well know, there are different levels and types of pain. I have no research, quotes, or statistics to back my belief that loneliness is one of the more painful types of pains, just a keen awareness that I hate feeling it. If you've ever suffered a wound to the heart from the arrow of loneliness, you know the pain I am describing.

You sit there alone, alone in your thoughts, alone in your pain, alone. The only companion that seems to befriend you is the voice that constantly reminds you of how alone you are, as if you weren't aware. It reminds you of how you got to that place, of the mistakes you've made, of the pains you've endured. It replays the lowlights of your life over and over, convincing you that, no, you shouldn't leave the house, the cubicle, or your isolation room. Staying home and staying put is the better option. History has taught you others can't be trusted. The voice whispers in disgust, "You're no better. You can't be trusted either." Alone you sit, only to hear the voice replay over and over again the joys of isolation.

Isolated was how I felt.

Trust

In case you forgot, I had destroyed all my previous friendships with my choices. I had moved. I had started a new job and was alone in a new place both occupationally and relationally. I was standing on what felt like ridiculously shaky ground spiritually, if I was standing on any ground at all. Things with God seemed to be looking up, but I still had so far to go.

I was alone in this new world, and the reality I was facing was hard. Like the new kid standing in the doorway of the cafeteria on the first day of school, I stood there in the doorway of my life paralyzed, wondering, Who will my friends be? Who should I try to talk to? Will I be able to make new friends in this new place? Do I try to make new ones just like my old ones?

A thought crept into my mind that if I sought out the same type of friends I'd been running with before, I'd end up running down that old path again. I knew where that path led—nowhere, and it got there fast. This new way, I felt, required new friends. But I was stuck. My experiences had told me church people couldn't be trusted, but I couldn't be trusted with my old friends. I felt overwhelmed as I considered the risk.

Why risk? Why feel overwhelmed? Nah, let's not do anything dramatic like that. Let's not and say we did. Instead, how about we do what we do best? Yep, why be brave and participate in life when you can isolate? Yes, isolation! That will turn out better.

If AIDS was the epidemic plaguing our country in the '80s and '90s, isolation is the disease wreaking havoc on people and culture today. We isolate behind our illuminated screens with too-busy-for-others lives and starve relationally for real connection and meaning. We are a country without community, and it's taken its toll.

Harvard professor Robert D. Putnam discusses this epidemic of isolation that he calls "declining social capital" in his book *Bowling Alone*: "The very fabric of our connections with each other has plummeted, impoverishing our lives and communities."[3] Now if that's too wordy for you, let me break it down into simple English. Putnam said that the greatest social epidemic in American life is loneliness, and loneliness hurts us.

Peter Block, in his book *Community: The Structure of Belonging*, echoes Putnam's thoughts:

> The absence of belonging is so widespread that we might say we are living in an age of isolation, imitating the lament from early in the last century, when life was referred to as the age of anxiety. Ironically, we talk today of how small our world has become, with the shrinking effect of globalization, instant sharing of information,

quick technology, workplaces that operate around the globe. Yet these do not create a sense of belonging. They provide connection, diverse information, an infinite range of opinion. But all this does *not* create the connection *from* which we can become grounded and experience the sense of safety that arises from a place where we are emotionally, spiritually, and psychologically a member.[4]

This lack of belonging begs a question: Why do we do it? Why do we live so isolated? You hate it. I hate it. Why did I do it then? Why am I so often tempted to live isolated now?

Let's hit pause on the DVR and come back to that question in a bit. I'd like for you to ponder this question first: Does God ever seem cruel to you or seem to ask too much?

Bargaining with God

Before some of you Jesus fans jump ship and stop reading the book, I am not intending to plant ideas, speak words of heresy, or be a Negative Nancy. I'm used to being in a "come as you are" culture, which means I often show up with the tough questions I am wrestling with or the hard emotions surrounding the answers I've been given. Can I be honest and wrestle in front of you for a second?

I propose the above question because sometimes what God asks me to do just feels like too much. It's too hard. Bearing that cross is too heavy. It looks like it will crush me or, at the least, impale me with a really bad splinter.

The next nudge I felt from God seemed as though it was too much, too heavy. Timothy Keller's words in *Counterfeit Gods* let me know he gets it: "Sometimes God seems to be killing us when he's actually saving us."[5] This next request felt too cruel and that it might just be the end of me. How dare he ask me to be that vulnerable? Under the suffocating loneliness that blanketed me, I felt him nudge me to get up and step forward, down the way of community into new community—church people community.

Ugh. I'd rather stay curled up here in my misery, thank you very much.

Again, I swallowed the taste from the vinegar-soaked dill pickle I had put in my mouth when I agreed to do whatever he asked for a year. So bravely I bargained (really, just begged). I let God know that because I'd been so brave to actually attend a church, the least he could do for me was give me one friend. That's all I asked—one person I could sit with in the cafeteria at lunch as I ate from my Strawberry Shortcake lunch box. (Kidding about the cafeteria/lunch box part, but you get the idea. Like the new kid at school, I just wanted a friend.) And he provided one.

Her name is Karin. You've probably met her or are Facebook friends with her or know someone who knows her or is Facebook friends with her. She's got a million of them, or something close to that. She's like that, one of those people everyone knows and everyone likes, for good reason. She's really nice and really positive, all the time.

She drives a blue VW convertible bug that's supercute, and she likes life to be fun and lives it adventurously. She was the first person God put in my life as I walked down this new way. Blonde, bright, and brilliant, she scared the crap out of me.

We met in a class at church on a Sunday afternoon. We sat next to each other at one of those big, round, uncomfortable tables designed so you have to talk. She started talking to me. I stared back, panicky, trying to figure out why she was talking to *me* and racking my brain for a "normal" church person response. I was rusty on my "top 100 churchie answers to give when at church." I pulled the "fake it 'til you make it" card out and must have done a good job, because she asked me for my number. She said she wanted to hang out—with me. My mind couldn't comprehend it.

That might sound odd, but picture a perfectly normal-looking, Jesus-loving, just-off-the-mission-field-in-Spain nice girl. That was Karin. Me, on the other hand, well, you've read what I had been up to. What I felt about me shouldn't be mixing with what I believed to be true about her. Oil doesn't mix with vinegar. And I definitely felt like vinegar. But I thought I didn't have much to worry about, because I was sure she would forget or lose my number or not call for a thousand other reasons I normally give when I forget or fail to call someone back.

But she didn't forget. She called a day or two later. And I did what every scared-to-death, no-clue-what-to-do avoider does: I didn't answer. I know, I know, but before you judge me for not answering on purpose, hear me out. I was scared, and I normally don't ever answer calls. I let them go to voice mail and then call back or text the answer later.

So I let it go to voice mail and waited to see what type of message a Jesus princess would leave for an ugly duckling like me (just honest interior thoughts here, people). As the message began, it seemed simple enough: "Hi Melissa! This is Karin! That you met at Gateway! I was calling to see if you wanted to hang out! Maybe grab dinner! Talk!"

First off, yes, Karin often leaves messages and talks with an exclamation point at the end of every sentence. She's one of those excited, encouraging, positive, every-day-is-sunny kind of people. That was frightening enough. But did you catch what she said that truly scared the banana off my banana split? She wanted to grab dinner—and talk?!

This scared me to death. I wasn't worried that I would be attracted to her. Ninety-nine percent of the women I've known I have felt zero attraction toward. So it's not something I worried about then or now. But I was terrified to take a step toward friendship. I ignored her call, and the next one. I think she actually called three or four times to hang out before something in me (to this day I don't know what) finally said okay.

We went to the Sunday evening service at church and then went out for a burger at Mighty Fine (which, if you're ever in Austin, is a great place to go for a good burger). What I feared most happened. She asked me about me—who I was, where I'd come from, how I'd gotten to Gateway, how long I had liked Jesus, blah, blah, blah. She asked all the questions I didn't want to answer to Polly Perfect Princess. I sat across that table, though, and I felt God nudge me to tell her the truth.

She was the real test. After all, it's easy for a church to say "come as you are," but do they really mean it when a person is not just an impressive additional number in the pew but a real-life, in-your-face person sitting in front of you telling her story? A story that includes sin and shame and then more sin and a no-clue, don't-think-I-could-ever-trust-you heart behind it.

I told her about my life, about my lifestyle. I dropped it right there between the ketchup and my fries. She didn't flinch. I don't remember exactly what she said. Mainly, I remember that she listened, and she smiled, and then she invited me to hang out again, and then again, and again.

She just kept inviting me to things—church things, social things, normal people things with actual people whom she'd introduce me to: other pretty-pretty princesses and boys, men. She introduced me to them too, which terrified me. I hadn't done the guy thing in almost a decade. I'm not talking dating; I mean simply as friends, acquaintances. Back in the day, it wasn't cool or kosher to have gay friends in the way society embraces today, so I had been living an all-female lifestyle in an all-female community while working in an almost all-female profession. I was rarely around guys, and if I was, they were either gay guys or male coaches.

I would get invited to parties at which boys would be in attendance. Now, consider the issue: I used to dress like a guy to avoid having to talk to guys, or anyone else really. I had no clue what I was supposed to wear or how I was supposed to act or what I was supposed to say.

I pause here to interject again that I had no clue where I was on the map in relation to my sexuality. I wasn't trying to not be gay or be straight or fix this or that. I was trying to figure out God, period, not my gender or my sexuality. What's fascinating is how much of our gender and sexuality gets wrapped up in how we dress. Think about it. I can dress in a heterosexual, homosexual, asexual, metrosexual, overly sexual, or transsexual way.

We dress to attract. We dress to repel and avoid. We do it with clothes. We do it with our bodies. Just head into your local gym or health club to see the using-my-body-to-attract addicts, or hear the pain of some of my dear friends who have confided that they can't stop overeating because they, subconsciously or not, use the extra weight to repel guys in order to stay safe and not run the risk of attracting more sexual abuse into their lives.

Attract, repel. How do you dress when you only want to attract God?

I didn't want to attract any church people into my life, but I also didn't want to repel them. I just wanted God and a couple of friends who would not get in the way.

Imagine a scared little girl standing in front of her closet, crying, lost on what to wear—except she's thirty-four. I'm not asking, "Do I wear the peach blouse with sleeves or the teal one without?" That's not "lost" on what to wear. (I've been that girl too, and there's a difference.) Maybe there isn't a way to explain it to you if you haven't struggled with your sexuality or your gender. Your insides and your outsides don't match, and you don't know who to listen to. And those are just the critics inside your head.

Here's the issue with walking the way of community. Communities are made up of people. People have opinions; people judge. Communities of people come with hidden rules and membership requirements. Some even have secret handshakes and a secret language, even in the church (or should I say especially in the church?). Would my tattoos and not-know-what-to-do style of dress get me kicked out before I was even let in?

My first steps down the way of community were exhausting. But I kept stepping, and God kept nudging. Karin kept asking, and I kept finding something to wear, even though, to this day, I can't remember what that first outfit was. Slowly I began to have them—friends.

What a fairy-tale story, eh? The frightened prodigal loner finds friends. (The cynic in me is rolling my eyes.) If only it were that easy. It wasn't.

Dragons are never slain without a fight, except it wasn't just a fight. A hundred battles were fought in my closet. Thousands of them were fought in my head. Even more were fought in my heart.

The reality? The way of community is hard. It comes with an invitation that feels like an execution. The invitation? Live connected.

Live Connected

I didn't want to live connected (said in a sarcastic tone with more rolling of the eyes). I had tried that before. I got hurt; I got burned. I had dressed and played the game, and at the end of the day, I had lost. Karin was nice, so were a few others, but I wanted to keep them at arm's length to stay safe, if I even let them that close at all.

Then came another nudge with an almost silent whisper: "Live connected with your heart." Again, he sometimes asks too much, or so I often feel. Sitting here today, overlooking the green field and the pond recently refreshed by the summer rain, I know the nudge was what I needed. I wouldn't have made it here alone.

I want to tell those reading this who are living in the land of isolation that I get it. I get why you're there. It's hard to live connected and walk the way of community. It's hard. It's scary. It's exhausting. It feels like death. Honestly, if your story is anything like mine, it will be all those things.

Living connected feels like death and will bring death to you if you let it—death to your fears, death to your misperceptions, death to your self-defeating games. And death birthing new life—a new perspective, new relationships, a new love, a new you. Jesus talks about this when he says to the crowd, "If anyone would come after me, let him deny himself and take up his cross daily and follow me. For whoever would save his life will lose it, but whoever loses his life for my sake will save it" (Luke 9:23–24).

Deny what I want. Take up a cross. Follow death. I know. It would make for a lousy brochure, yet it works. His invitation when accepted, his directions when followed—they work.

Those PBMs

I was connected to Karin. Karin was connecting me to others. She had invited me to attend a small group with her. I didn't want to go. I felt like it would suck, but I went, and it did.

Imagine a white Tahoe sitting outside a two-story brick house in a nice neighborhood. The sky is dark from the winter evening hours. It's almost 7:00 p.m., which I believe to be the mandatory starting time for all small groups to begin. I watch one beautiful woman after another get out of her car and walk in. I wanted to get out of the car and run down the street with scissors. That seemed less risky.

Karin had invited me to a women's small group being held at the pastor's house. His wife was one of the leaders. All of the ladies were PBMs. You might not know that self-created acronym, so let me explain. PBM stands for Pottery Barn Mom. That's my way of describing the group of ladies in this group. All of them, besides Karin, were married. Strike one. They all had kids. Strike two. They all were beautiful, and they all looked as if they had just gotten off the set of *Sex in the City* or *Real Housewives*. Strike three.

I was out, except I wasn't. God wanted me, the gay ugly duckling, to walk in and spend two hours having polite biblical conversation with these PBMs—moms who looked like they had it all together and spent their days shopping at Pottery Barn so they could go home and decorate their perfect lives.

I sat in my car and prayed—to be abducted by aliens, or to have an instantaneous twenty-four-hour flu hit me, or leprosy, anything so I wouldn't have to get out of my Tahoe and walk the twenty-six steps toward that front door into the land of Beauty when I felt like Beast. I think I even got so desperate that I simply prayed for Jesus to return at that moment.

In case you're curious, he didn't.

Instead, I sat in my car with a death-like grip on the steering wheel and tears streaming down my face, uttering, "If you want me to go in there, you are going to have to get me out of this car, because I am not going!" Somehow he won. I released my grip and opened the door. My body obeyed him while my mind screamed, "Traitor!"

I did it. I went in and faced the tidal wave of panic, insecurity, and fear. I hated every second of it, seriously.

That continued week after week. Wednesday nights would come with me sitting outside their house, begging God, crying, only to find myself walking up to the front door again.

Why?

No Clue

Why would God ask me to live connected with women so different from me as I traveled down the way of community? Why would God ask me to do life with people nothing like me? Why might he ask you to do the same?

My answer? We don't know what we need. We aren't as smart as we think we are. The author of Proverbs echoes this truth. God has a better perspective on our lives than we do:

> Trust in the LORD with all your heart,
>   and do not lean on your own understanding.
> In all your ways acknowledge him,
>   and he will make straight your paths. (Prov. 3:5–6)

These oft-stitched and monogrammed verses are a favorite for many, but I have to pause here and say, I hated these verses. Trusting

God was hard, and I happened to be pretty fond of leaning on my own understanding. After all, I knew me. I spent a lot of time with me. I got to hear quite often how I felt. I was pretty aware of what I wanted. I had a college degree. I knew what I needed.

God gently and politely shook his head and said no. You don't have a clue what you need. Ouch. I swallowed that dose of medicine as I acknowledged he was right. I didn't.

When every part of me would crave to connect and do life with people just like me, God reminded me I'd already tried that. Birds of a feather flock together, right? I had been flying with people just like me. I hadn't flown very far. I hadn't flown anywhere at all, actually, just in circles. God, in his divine plan, called me to dive into community with people not like me.[6] He didn't seem to care that I didn't like people not like me.

Different was difficult. I'd had enough difficulty in my life already. I didn't need church acquaintances adding more difficulty. Here's the rub: I had my perspective on this, and God had his. Who was right? Who would I heed and listen to? Proverbs interjects here, "In all your ways acknowledge him."

For you language nerds, *all* in Hebrew means the same as it does in Greek. All means *all*. All includes my relationships, my friendships, my community, my sexuality. All means God gets a say—in all of it.

He nodded a direction and I was supposed to step that way, even if it was something as difficult as stepping into a room full of beautiful, accomplished women. This is a tough concept. We don't like being told what to do, do we? We are Americans, and we have rights, personal rights, like the right to pursue happiness. What would make me happy, God, is not to be in a group with those kinds of women.

Choosing the Outcome

You might not be able to readily relate. A room full of Pottery Barn Moms or a breakfast meeting with the GGBG (Godly Guys

Business Group) might be right up your alley. Those might be your peeps, and you might be as comfy there as plum jelly on a homemade biscuit.

Imagine, then, if God wanted a gay guy or girl to do life in your group. How would that fly? Or a black man, a Muslim, or a stripper? Or some pretty type that was pressed and polished? Would that mess up your easy conversational flow? Would your Facebook group selfies be reconsidered if someone different from you joined in?

Here's a question I'd like you to ponder: Who really chooses your community for you?

Let's press further. Think for a moment. What's the last choice God was allowed to make for you? Really?

If I am honest, I am not really a good picker. I mean, I can pick my nose pretty well; we've established that. But past that, my deceitful heart will always want to pick what is easy and self-serving. When I pick what is self-serving, it doesn't serve anyone, and especially not me.

What if we didn't choose? What if we acknowledged him in all things and let him choose? What would be the outcome?

Scripture says God will make my path straight. He will make yours straight too. What's your crooked issue? What's the issue or area you, like a drunk struggling to walk the yellow line, have been failing to walk correctly? What area do you need him to straighten out? What if you gave him permission to do whatever he wanted to in your life in whatever order he wanted to do it? What if that permission meant he asked you to step into a new community, or if you have previously run away from godly community, what if he invited you to come back home—to them, to him?

Imagine letting go of all control. Imagine letting him lead you into the community that's best for you, the community that will grow the best fruit in you. It's a guarantee. If you stick around long enough and don't bail, living connected will grow you. It will change you, transform you, and most of all free you—from yourself.

The truth: transformation never occurs in isolation.

Before we look more closely at the benefits of community, let me pause to clarify my definition of community. Community isn't just showing up at a regular small group gathering with fried pickles (which is my favorite food item to bring to my group's gathering). It's not about the food. Community is being fully known and knowing others fully. It's letting them love the parts of you that you don't like, and it's loving the unlovely parts of them.

Did you catch that? Being fully known. In Gateway terms, we call that the last 10 percent. To have true community means that you are connected with people who have earned the right, through integrity and authenticity, to know the last 10 percent of your heart, your mind's thoughts, and your life.

This level of transparency will be discussed further in the next chapter, but it's vital when walking down the way of community. The destination of this way is transparent, Spirit-led, Spirit-filled relational community. This is vital, because if I am never able to be fully known, I can never be fully loved. If the dark parts of my heart never have the opportunity to be touched by the light of someone's sacrificial love on behalf of Jesus, I will remain enslaved. Put simply: when someone knows the worst of me and still sticks around to love me, that changes me. That's grace in the flesh.

Like an American Express membership, community has its privileges, so let's look at the benefits.

Benefit #1: Community Comforts Us

I have a dear friend who was brave and followed God's leading to open a bakery. For three years, while the bakery was open, I had the blessing of getting to work behind the counter, learning how to decorate cakes and cookies, as well as playing cashier for all the sugar addicts and excited little ones who came in the door.

What I most enjoyed about working there was the first three seconds of walking in the door. Oh, the smell! Is there anything better than the aroma of cakes, pies, and cookies in the oven? I think that's what heaven will smell like! Freshly baked chocolate chip cookies!

What I loved most about the smell coming from the oven was the promise of the yumminess that would come next. The aroma always preceded the blessing, which is a powerful thought. Aroma precedes blessing. For Christ-followers, we are that aroma. We precede the blessing—the blessing is Christ. "For we are the aroma of Christ to God among those who are being saved and among those who are perishing, to one a fragrance from death to death, to the other a fragrance from life to life" (2 Cor. 2:15–16).

Our souls need the fragrant offering of something new and wonderful. The fragrance of Christ is just that—the new and the wonderful. We are the aroma to each other, reminding each other that something better is on the way. The fragrance of Christ in us has the power to refresh and restore a tired soul searching for something to lift his or her spirit. We are that provision. If you've ever walked into a bakery, you know how potent the comforting smell of chocolate and gluten-filled carbohydrates can be. Walking into a fragrant community of Christ-followers can be just the same—comforting.

Don't we all need comfort? It's a tough world. We get hurt, banged, and bruised. We bleed and, as we've discussed, we often bleed alone. Sometimes we just need a hug, a real one, from a father or mother we live too far away from. Maybe our whole lives have been spent apart, and the pain of never knowing a father's hug gnaws at our souls.

I hear this often when I walk alongside others as they take steps of faith. In the rough parts of the journey, I hear them say, "I just wish I could feel God hug me or hold me, literally." I know this feeling too well, as I used to say and feel the same way. For many of you like me, touch has wounded us. I needed a comforting, safe touch to restore me. I needed it from God. I didn't want it from people, yet God uses people—like Jeff.

Jeff is an amazing man of God whom I met a few years ago while attending a weekend retreat. After an intensely hard exercise in which I was working through some trust issues I had with God the Father, I was undone. I was carnally aware of how badly I needed a Father's hug—not a mother's hug, nor a friend's hug, nor a hug from an overly sensitive people pleaser or gifted empathetic soul. I needed a strong yet tender hug full of power and protection. I needed a hug from God the Father. I had no recollection of ever feeling what my heart was desiring, but I was aware I needed it. I opened up the possibility in a feeble, under-my-breath prayer to God. "Please, God. Can you use someone in this room to hug me like you would? If you see me and hear me, I know you have the ability to do this."

In the next activity, we were to partner with someone. I found myself standing beside Jeff. During the activity, the most amazing thing happened. Jeff hugged me, but it wasn't him; it was God. God was hugging me. I can't describe in words how the transformation occurred, but I was overwhelmed. I felt as if a new dimension entered my soul as I was hugged by my heavenly Father, using this man as a vessel.

That's the tragedy. When I avoid community, I take away the Spirit's opportunity to use people as vessels for the love he wants to give me. I easily neuter the Lion and disregard the Lamb when I disregard his people. When I disregard authenticity in community, I block all ability for the deepest hurts and wounds I have to receive the comforting light of love they so desperately need.

So, friend, do you need comfort too? How about encouragement? Would having someone in your corner, who actually knew the opponent you were facing in the ring, help you slay him? What about a whole community of people cheering your name? "Let us consider how to stir up one another to love and good works, not neglecting to meet together, as is the habit of some, but encouraging one another, and all the more as you see the Day drawing near" (Heb. 10:24–25). See the pattern? Hang out regularly. Don't forget. Be honest about what you need cheering for. Let people cheer you on. Do it more and more as we get closer to the day.

Solomon echoes these thoughts in Ecclesiastes 4: "Two are better than one, because they have a good reward for their toil. For if they fall, one will lift up his fellow. But woe to him who is alone when he falls and has not another to lift him up!" (vv. 9–10). That's comforting to me, having people in my corner who can pick me up. You might say, "Well, Melissa, I have good friends who are comforting and know how to pick me up when I am down. What's the big deal about having community within the church? It might have helped you, but why do I need it?"

Glad you asked.

Benefit #2: Community Carves Us

Yep, I said it. Community carves us. It carves, as with a knife.

I am impressed with it too. Maybe you're not so impressed. Maybe you're more alarmed, hopefully not to the point you've abandoned ship. Keep reading and let me explain.

There were things in my life at the time that weren't working for me. I mean, who sits outside of a house crying every Wednesday night because other women are in it? I had wounds, fears, insecurities, and habits that had me roadblocked and stuck in my own life. As John Burke so perfectly puts it, there was a lot of mud on the masterpiece.

Actually, I don't think mine was mud. It was more like clay that had been there so long it had turned into stone. Stuck like a statue, that was me, and if you don't know much about statues, they aren't very good at unsticking themselves. Even in Disney movies, it takes magic dust or Aslan's breath to melt someone frozen in ice or stone.

John Ortberg says in *The Me I Want to Be*, "God uses people to form people."[7] God used those women and my attendance in that first group to chisel away the bitter chip I used to carry on my shoulder. These were obviously beautiful women, comfortable in their femininity, and I hated them for it. I would spend all my energy judging them and making up horrible stories in my head to validate my desire to reject them. Get them before they get me! That was my subconscious motto, 'til one day, while driving home from a Wednesday night gathering, God revealed to me what I had been doing. The women weren't rejecting me; I was rejecting them, giving them the Heisman stiff-arm as I drove away. I heard the chink-chink-chink as the chip was chiseled away, as I let my heart absorb the truth and repent. For you nonchurch folks, don't let the word *repent* ruffle your feathers. It just means to change your mind. My thoughts were wrong, and I needed to be thinking God's thoughts about those women. They were nice, and I needed to give them the chance to be that.

More chiseling occurred as I accepted the invitation to become "running" partners with Karin and a woman in the group named Sarah. I was starting to feel a little safe with Karin. This Sarah woman, on the other hand, made me all sorts of uncomfortable with her perfect this and beautiful that. The whole running partner concept unnerved me. Being in a living room with up to twelve other women was bad enough, but now they wanted us to start meeting in twos or threes so we could share more? Hold each other accountable? Spiritually "run" together? I didn't even physically run with other people because it was too vulnerable, much less spiritually! No thank you!

Then came the nudge. Go. Meet with them.

It was horrible. We met every other week to share our answers to our homework in the "Morph: Love God"[8] study that had us look at how we view God. Great study and all, but in no way did I want to share my answers with those two! I was the gay girl sharing with the pretty, pretty princesses! Please! At least in a group of up to twelve you can still hide. With only two others, there wasn't any hiding! Aauuggh!

This story reminds me of one of my roommate's dogs, Little Bit. Little is a Boston terrier and is full of life, especially when she is snoring. I've never heard a dog snore so loudly. She's cute, except for one flaw: she won't hold still when you try to clip her nails. She tries to bite or head butt you. We've been able to clip a total of only two nails since she moved in. To my point, the other nails are so long I call her Edward Scissorpaws. If only we could communicate to her that we aren't trying to hurt her; we are just trying to trim away the excess that isn't good for her.

That's how I felt inside as I met with Sarah and Karin. I wanted to run, bite, claw, or head butt them or God—anything other than be still and endure what would ultimately be good for me.

Somehow, I got through it. I went every other week to Sarah's house and, though I felt nauseated, was able to share some of my answers. They didn't reject me. In fact, what those weeks together did for me was huge. They opened the door for this verse to become pivotal and true in my life: "As iron sharpens iron, so one person sharpens another" (Prov. 27:17 NIV). Having to dig deeper into my heart and reveal truth to my spiritual running partners sharpened me then and has been sharpening me ever since.

People living in godly community will do that. They will poke into areas of your life so light can enter in. This is not done in a nosey, boundary-less, gossipy way, but those in godly community will follow the Spirit's leading. They will speak God's Word when led. Notice I said when led. Jesus knew all of the Scriptures when he walked on earth, but as he walked alongside others, his first words were often questions. Those in godly community will work to be good listeners and not drive-by Scripture slingers. Our job in community is to be gentle as we do life with each other. Paul says, "Dear brothers and sisters, if another believer is overcome by some sin, you who are godly should gently and humbly help that person back onto the right path. And be careful not to fall into the same temptation yourself" (Gal. 6:1 NLT).

Yes, allowing godly counsel into your life can be difficult. God will give other people in your community words to share with you. They will ask you questions you don't want to answer. They will make mistakes. I've yet to make it through a year without wanting to hit my running partners, literally. I'm really not a violent person! They just make me angry when they ask questions about things I don't want to look at. I'd rather live in the land of self-protection and denial. It's much easier there. But I don't grow there; I don't get chiseled; I don't transform; I don't mature. As Larry Crabb says in *Inside Out*, "The mark of maturity is love, and the essence of love is relating without self-protection."[9]

We have to be brave enough to step into community without self-protecting (letting God be our protector) and with a willingness to grow and transform. We also have to be people willing to speak loving truth when need be. Community is a give-and-take experience. I have to be willing to receive tough truth as well as give it, and giving it can be just as hard.

Paul felt this tension when he was addressing the Galatians about old patterns they were falling back into. He proposed the question midtalk, "Have I then become your enemy by telling you the truth?" (Gal. 4:16).

Paul was in the middle of addressing the Galatians about some bad choices and the anger it was bringing up in them. I hate to admit it, but I can be just as bad as the Galatians and fall back into my own playlist of bad habits. To make matters worse, not only am I a poor chooser, but I am also likely to think my way is the right way. My choices, because I make them in all my glorious, profound wisdom, will be (I think) the right move for me to make. My pride and ego like to be right, think I am right, and prove to those objecting why they are wrong. I too easily self-protect. I too easily play the fool. "The way of a fool is right in his own eyes, but a wise man listens to advice" (Prov. 12:15).

How many times have I played the fool when making choices? Too many to count, and you've already read about some of them and their effects. But God's invitation back into godly community changed that trajectory. I was able to trade the life of a fool for a chance at wisdom. But I had to be humble enough to accept truth. I had to be willing to take in feedback. And most of us, if we are honest, like to surround ourselves with "yes men." Scripture speaks to the difference: "Wounds from a friend can be trusted, but an enemy multiplies kisses" (Prov. 27:6 NIV).

Your friends and your community really matter. As secular studies show, if you want to see what you will look or be like in the next five to ten years, just look at your five closest friends. They are the number one indicator of what you will be like in the future. Do your friends avoid the tough stuff and let you stay stagnant? Do they challenge you? Are you at a point where you want more in life? Try a new community. Pray for it. Hear the advice from Solomon speaking thousands of years ago: "Whoever walks with the wise becomes wise, but the companion of fools will suffer harm" (Prov. 13:20).

Benefit #3: Community Covers Us

I have friends in law enforcement who often talk of having my 6. Do you know this term? It means they have your back. In law enforcement and military terms, where lives are often on the line, someone having your 6 can mean the difference between you making it home in the car you came in or heading away from a scene in an emergency vehicle, or worse.

Life in the field "spiritually" is just as dangerous, if not more. As we've discussed, Satan is intent on stealing, killing, and destroying anything good in your life. Your life is being lived in the middle of a war. It's easy to miss that fact, since most of what we fight[10] we can't see. This invisible war has raged on around you since the day you were born. If, for a moment, the war could become visible, how would you respond? Would you plan? Would you prepare? Would you fight? How would you fight? What would you do first, second, and third?

Who would you enlist to fight with you? What would your weapon of choice be? Proverbs has some advice for you to consider: "For by wise guidance you can wage your war, and in abundance of counselors there is victory" (24:6). Proverbs 11:14 backs that up: "Where there is no guidance, a people falls, but in an abundance of counselors there is safety." Victory and safety found in godly community. Nice.

For you lone-ranger types, here's the warning: the sheep living away from the flock is always the easiest for the wolf to pick off. The truth I believe God wants you to hear is that you can't make it alone. "We need others because of the command to reproduce and subdue; and its New Testament companion, the Great Commission, cannot be carried out by any one person. God's glory is displayed in a corporate body more fully than it is in individuals. Image-bearers are not lone rangers."[11]

Did you see that? Image-bearer—that's me. I was made in his image. You were too. Do you believe it? If you are like me, that's been the biggest challenge, because I never felt it. I never felt beautiful, never felt loved, never felt worthy. The only thing I felt I was worth was leaving. That's what I believed to be true. That's what I came into godly community believing. I believed I was worth leaving, and I spent my first days, months, and maybe even years waiting to be left.

Have you ever done that? Sat around waiting for someone to leave? Maybe it was relatives leaving to go home, or an ex packing up stuff to leave when the relationship ended, or your child leaving to go to school. It's a weird experience, waiting to be left. It feels lonely, awkward. Your life is put on pause until the door closes, and you are then able to have that "what now" conversation with yourself.

I lived that way for a long while—waiting to be left, believing I was worthy of being left. But I wasn't. Karin stuck around. Believe me, I've given her plenty of reasons to leave. I have with others as well: Ericka, Holly, Ruth, Kristi, so many others. All have stayed and comforted, carved, and covered me.

Despite the pushing, pulling, kicking, and running I've done in the past seven years, godly community has covered me with its physical presence in my life, and that has done more to show me God's desire to be present in my life than I can find words for.

Lastly, godly community covers me with truth: the truth of who I am in Christ, of God's love for me, of my calling and purpose. I'm covered with their counsel when they see me heading toward danger. I am covered with their presence, covered with their prayers, covered with truth—covered.

Are you convinced? God, the ultimate divine community who modeled it during creation, is inviting you into it. Jesus modeled it with his disciples. The early church seemed to nail it, and us? Well, we struggle with it, don't we?

Community has its benefits, as I've mentioned. I also acknowledge it comes with a cost. Pride will make you hate it. Shame will make you avoid it. The voices that will try to convince you to avoid the risk will be many. J. Keith Miller speaks to his experience in facing the battle of risk and shame:

> First, I had to find a place where I could see integrity in action, where it was safe to risk being open. I needed a context in which I could tell my own truth as I discovered it, and where I could test my new trust in God. . . . To my surprise, as I listened and began to share as vulnerably as I was comfortable sharing, I realized something incredible about the shaming voices. The only power they have, the only weapon in the shaming voices' arsenal with which to cripple our self-esteem and integrity, is the threat of revealing the shameful acts, character defects, and attitudes of our past. Psychologists have long known that our secrets control us. But when we voluntarily share these secrets in a spiritual community, the content we share and the power of the voices to shame us lose their strength. Eventually, to me, the shaming voices seemed to get weaker.[12]

Community is the Jesus with skin on that is willing to sit with you, even when you don't want to sit with yourself. With it, the rooms of your heart have the opportunity to be illuminated with love, which can silence the voices that mock and laugh. Yes, the risk is real. So is the reward. How do I know? I've experienced it. It's easier to find than you think.

Real community happens at the foot of the cross. Try it out. You just might find Jesus there.

8

The Way of Work

Feelings that are buried are always buried alive.

Larry Townsend[1]

Two blind men walked down a dirt road. Sounds like the opening line of a bad joke.

While not the opening line of a joke, it is the opening line of a story, a true story at that (see Matt. 9:27–31). The men were blind. The road was made of dirt. It was probably dusty, possibly difficult to navigate, especially difficult for two blind men. The distance they traveled isn't clear, but their mode of transportation is. They walked. Actually, they followed Jesus.

He had been at a ruler's house, hanging out, doing the normal everyday Jesus-y things that he did, like raising a ruler's daughter from the dead. Jesus finished up another death-to-life miracle and left the ruler's house to head home. (Home is used loosely because Jesus traveled a lot, so home was whatever house he was invited to for the night.) Somewhere in between the two houses, the blind men appeared on the dirt road, crying, loudly, repeating their cries over and over again, "Son of David! Son of David! Have mercy on us!"

Jesus's response? He kept on walking.

Yep. Jesus kept walking, right on by. He wasn't deaf, so it has to make you wonder. If Jesus heard them, why did he just keep walking? His seeming disregard had to communicate to them and to others: he's done for the night. He may be God, but he's still in a need-sleep body. He had called it a day and was headed to the place he was staying for the night, leaving the blind men standing there, alone, with their shouting and their tears.

The blind men, though, didn't stop. They kept going. They kept walking, stalking, begging, and crying out to Jesus. They ignored the ignoring and kept this up all the way to the house where Jesus sat inside. After all, it's a little hard to keep up with Jesus when you are blind. You have to take slower, safer steps. You probably have to stop to ask for help from time to time. Yet still, they walked on. Right up to and through the front door to where Jesus sat.

I imagine the blind men catching their breaths as they stood before him. I imagine the stares from the others inside the home, sitting around the table, listening to Jesus. I imagine their looks of disgust at the unwelcome intrusion. I imagine looks of curiosity on the faces of others as they wondered what Jesus would do. His response, though, I don't have to imagine. I know, thanks to Matthew documenting it so long ago.

This story from old intersects your story and mine today. This too-important story carries with it the vital question every traveler must answer on the way of hope. Jesus's question to the blind men? "Do you believe that I am able to do this?" (Matt. 9:28 NIV).

Ten simple words, yet they are the ten most important words, I believe, of this book. So let's read them again. "Do you believe that I am able to do this?"

The question asked of two beggars over two thousand years ago is the same question Jesus asks us today. The only difference lies in the "this." It makes me wonder. What is your "this"?

The beggars wanted sight, obviously. Me? I want to finish this book, obviously. You? What do you want? What would you do to get it?

The blind men begged. They didn't take no for an answer. They endured criticism. They endured shame. They risked rejection. They endured pain. They didn't quit. They believed.

Belief is powerful.

Never Could, Never Will

I've recently been reminded of the power of believing. It happened a couple of weeks ago, when I was getting ready to leave on a writing trip. Some fleeting thought went through my head as I was packing my car that I should take my guitar with me. The randomness of this thought was comical, because my guitar had been sitting untouched in my room for over nine months, maybe even a year. I was given it by a friend who didn't want it anymore, and I hadn't touched it since receiving it.

After all, why should I touch it? I didn't play the guitar, never had been able to. I'd tried once or twice before and . . . nothing. It didn't take. A moment or two of humiliation and frustration and down the guitar went.

This random thought caught my full attention and led me out the door with guitar in hand. But why take a guitar I didn't know how to play?

I arrived at the creek house and began the process of unpacking for a week of writing. I set the guitar next to the fireplace and after passing it a time or two had the thought, Why not? Why not pick it up and strum it a bit? A moment of strumming led to a sitcom worth of YouTube videos, and thirty minutes later, my fingertips were crying. (You guitar players might remember the pain of uncalloused fingertips.) The important point lies not in the pain of my fingertips but in what happened while acquiring it.

My belief was changed. My previous thought process went something like this: I can't play the guitar. I can't play anything. I couldn't even get past beginner level on Rock Band years ago, when it was the cool thing to do. Nope, I can't play the guitar. I never have been able to, never will.

It's kind of sad reading it, eh? I know. It felt a little Debbie Downer-ish writing it.

But again, those had been my thoughts. Yet in a short time, something unknown in me began to change, and that original little thought started to morph and gain traction: Could I learn to play the guitar?

The little light of this thought flickered and then morphed again: I could learn to play the guitar.

Then came the thought, I could be a guitar player, a real one, who could play a whole song, and a real song—not just "Twinkle, Twinkle Little Star" or "Mary Had a Little Lamb," even though those were good ones. I could learn to play a real worship song, or two, or why not a bunch? I could do that. Not only could I be a real guitar player . . . no, that thought won't do. I . . . I . . . I could be a *good* guitar player. I could do that!

Why not? Isn't the quote by Henry Ford true? "Whether you think that you can or you can't, you're usually right."[2] It's self-efficacy at its finest. If I can believe it, I can achieve it.

Psychologist Albert Bandura would be so proud! I changed my mind and believed I could play the guitar, and now I can! Isn't that how it goes, or is supposed to? Sorry to burst your bubble, Albert, but I don't think that's how it goes, not totally, anyway. Here's why.

There are a million things I thought I could do but can't, enough that I could write a separate book on just that. The second volume could be written on the things I thought I could never do but now can.

There seems to be less truth to Ford's statement than what I'd like to believe. After all, I like positivity and pull-up-your-boot-straps, get-it-done-type thinking. But sometimes my bootstraps break, and during a lot of rain my socks still get wet, despite my kick-down-the-door, get-'er-done cowgirl boots (that I don't really wear; Chacos are more my thing because I live in Texas and boots are hot). If I am honest, what I know to be true has nothing to do with whether I think I can or can't. That's really not the issue. It's a symptom of the problem.

The real issue in the success of my life isn't about what I believe I can do but what I believe Jesus can do.

Do You Believe?

If I was given permission to rework the sentence, it would say, "Whether you think that Jesus can or Jesus can't, you're usually right."

Isn't that true? Think about it. How do I act if I believe that Jesus can? I act like the two blind men. I ask. I persist. I follow. I beg. I position myself. I don't give up. I ask some more. I persevere until he answers me, until the need is met. I don't quit.

How do I act if I believe that he can't, or doesn't want to, or won't (because I know his thoughts so well . . .)? I quit asking. I give up. I get angry. I look for ways to get what I need (said in a sarcastic tone, as it's not usually something I need but instead just want). I do whatever is necessary to get what I want. As he gently knocks on the door, I open it and make a judgment call on his ability to deliver within the expected thirty-minute delivery time, and then slam the door back in his face as if he's a pizza delivery driver who didn't bring the right order.

Whether I believe that he can or he can't, I prove myself right. So I wonder about your "this" that I asked earlier. Do you believe he can? Seriously? Jesus is asking you today, "Do you believe that I am able to do this?"

Do you believe that I am able to heal your marriage?

Do you believe that I am able to help you get out of debt?

Do you believe that I am able to help you make friends?

Do you believe that I am able to help you forgive so reconciliation can occur?

Do you believe that I am able to restore your daughter?

Do you believe that I am able to heal your son?

Do you believe that I am able to lead you to a healthy spouse?

Do you believe that I am able to lead you to a new and better job?

Do you believe that I am able to heal your church?

Do you believe that I am able to save you from your addiction?

Do you believe that I am able to heal your depression?

Do you believe that I am able to forgive all your sins?

Do you? Do you believe that I am able?

I believe this is the most important question to be answered as you glance down and ponder *The Way of Work*. Do you believe that he is able?

Want to know if you really believe? Look at your actions. Look at where you spend your money. Take a glance at how you spend your time. Glance back at how you've been sleeping and eating. And when was the last time you took a Sabbath rest, or vacation, or turned your phone off? Audit your life and you will catch a glimpse of the answer to that question.

Still need more help? Try this question: What in your life actually requires faith? What area of your life requires God to come through in such a way that if he doesn't, well, you're in a pickle? Do you have such an area? Have you ever had an area of your life that you let go of and let God have total control over like Peter did? You stepped out of the boat and out of all sound reasoning and walked toward Jesus, while the waves of danger splashed at your feet.

Listen for a moment. Which area of your life is he knocking on the door of right now, or gently whispering through the door, "Let me have this one; I am able"?

As your forehead and your palms rest on the back of that closed door, know that I get it. Sometimes it seems too scary, too vulnerable. The one door you most want to protect, keep control of, or have the contents of go your way is the one door he seems to be knocking on. It just feels safer to keep it closed, locked, bolted.

It's easy to keep the door shut one more day, isn't it? Funny how one more day often turns into a decade or a life, as you glance around asking, "How did I end up here?" The locked doors of our lives never allow us to fully live. Instead, we exist. We become masters of escape. We live our lives loudly so that we don't have to really hear the whisper, "I am able."

As you wrestle with whether to open a locked door in your life, let me share about one in mine. It hits a tender spot . . . a very tender spot.

Was He Able?

The way of hope was birthed while leaning against my own closed door labeled sexuality that I had kept sealed shut for so long, sitting outside of it, feeling hopeless, not wanting anyone to touch it, open it, or walk through it, especially me. My attempts to navigate this door on my own terms, in my own way, had led me from being straight to being gay to simply being exhausted.

Holding a door closed gets tiring, especially one that was never meant to be shut. If it was to be opened, which way was it supposed to swing? I had never been able to get the door to swing in a way that really made me happy. Both ways, gay and straight, had left me wanting.

I didn't want to be alone the rest of my life. I wanted love. I wanted relationship. I knew I could only "date" God so long. There would eventually come a time when that wouldn't be enough, right? Isn't that what society and *Jerry Maguire* teach us—that we need a relationship to really be complete?

So I sat in my thoughts, running a risk analysis, if you will.

☑ God had been able to help me find a church,

☑ and new friends,

☑ and he was leading me,

☑ challenging me.

☑ In so many ways, I was seeing that he was listening

☑ and that he cared.

Dare I really believe that he was able to do something with my sexuality? This core part of who I was?

I sat with the question day after day. I replayed the stories spoken onstage at church by those three brave souls. He was able for them. Again, I questioned, was he able to do something good with my sexuality? After all, miracle stories in others' lives are great, except that they happen in *their* lives and not in mine. I needed something to happen for me—something, anything.

I couldn't have the door opened and make it every day with nothing changed. I couldn't go back to living in the gay lifestyle. Too much had begun changing in my heart. Even though parts of my heart and body still craved it deeply, I knew it wasn't what God wanted. Don't ask me the day I fully knew it. I think it's something I'd known all along. It was just a truth I didn't want to face. But if I couldn't be gay, how in the world could God ever get me "straight"—that girl who liked to dress like a boy. Was he able to heal my sexuality?

I believe this is the ultimate question for someone struggling with same-sex attraction. If I let God have this area of my life, will he heal it? Or will I struggle with desires the rest of my life? Can I ever be attracted to the opposite sex, and can they be attracted to me? Will heterosexual sex, if I ever get married, be fulfilling? Will I spend the rest of my life without someone and die alone? I didn't want to live or die alone.

Dying seemed easier than letting God inside that door and giving him a chance at healing me. If you don't ever give him a chance, you can't, or won't, be disappointed, right? I'd given him a chance in college when I'd cried out to him multiple times to kill the monster. As he had done with the blind men, Jesus just seemed to walk on by. He either didn't hear me or didn't care. Would he care now? Was he able and willing now?

This is comical to read now. I think God was ready back in college. I was the one who wasn't. I wasn't ready to let him in that door without stipulations and rules on what that healing would or could look like. It couldn't be messy. People couldn't know. I wanted him to heal me in a small, dark, hidden closet, while he wanted the space and air of my front lawn to do his work. Funny thing about God, he doesn't heal on demand, on command, or with limitations. I think that's what I tried to do in college. I wanted to demand or command him to heal my monster on my terms, but nothing public, please. Heal the monster without letting the monster see the light.

If I've learned anything, it's that deeds of the dark only get healed in the light and on God's terms, not necessarily my way or in my timing.

This reminds me of Naaman, the commander of the Syrian army. He and I were a lot alike—wanting healing our way, in our time, and in the process asking God, "Please don't step on our pride."

Look with me at 2 Kings chapter 5. Naaman, a mighty warrior, a leader of men, was in charge. I imagine him as a mix of Mel Gibson's character in *Braveheart* and Russell Crowe's character in *Gladiator*. He was strong, masculine, favored, and . . . possibly, wearing a kilt. Only one slight difference plagued Naaman's bravado. He had leprosy. In those days and now, leprosy wasn't the "in" thing, especially if you were the man in charge.

He had it, and he hated it. I can only imagine the shame he carried hidden while he rode high on his horse. After all, you can't let your men see you sweat, or suffer, or have a blister burst from the friction of your saddled horse. You can't have a down day because you hate your flesh and that day your flesh seems to hate you.

One day, hope came to Naaman. A servant girl from Israel was working in his home. She braved a conversation and said to Naaman's wife, "If only my master would see the prophet who is in Samaria! He would cure him of his leprosy" (2 Kings 5:3).

I often wonder how long it took Naaman's wife to take the news to him. Did she sprint out the door that second and interrupt him at work? Did she wait until later that night when he got home? If there had been so many failed attempts at healing, did she file it away a while as one more kooky cure that would fail? Me? I like to imagine she ran. That the hope sounded so hopeful she couldn't sit still. Those of you who are married, how long would you wait to share the news of possible healing with the one you love?

Naaman, upon hearing the news whenever or however it came from his wife, quickly took it to his boss, the king of Syria. He would need some time off from leading the army to pursue his healing out of town. Upon hearing the news, the king blessed him and said, "Go now," and sent Naaman to Israel with the necessary paperwork needed for such a trip.

After Naaman meets the king of Israel and works through a brief misunderstanding of the purpose of the trip, word makes it to Elisha, the prophet, that Naaman has come for healing. Elisha sends word and invites Naaman to head over to his place. Nice. A personal invitation for a personal healing. When Naaman arrives at Elisha's place with all his chariots and horses, Elisha sends out his messenger to meet him with instructions for his healing.

You read that right. Elisha sends his messenger. He doesn't even bother to come out. Now you might not understand the significance of this little action on Elisha's part, so let's put it into context. This would be like the vice president of the United States planning to meet with the pope and the pope sending out his chauffeur with the peace treaty on a clipboard to be signed because he was too busy.

In the world of prophets, politics, and power, you simply don't do that. The prideful and the powerful always get the pleasure of personal attention. But Elisha didn't play according to the world's standards.

The messenger gives the Post-it-note prescription for healing to Naaman that says, "Go, wash yourself seven times in the Jordan, and your flesh will be restored and you will be cleansed" (2 Kings 5:10 NIV). Excuse me? A Post-it note? From a messenger boy? Where is Elisha? He wants me to do what? Skinny dip seven times in a nasty creek? That's going to make me better? Is this a joke? Am I being punked? Is this some bad reality TV show?

Outraged, Naaman dismisses the messenger's words and turns to leave. He wants healing but not that way, not under those terms. After all, he is the commander of the Syrian army. Who does this small-town prophet think he is?

I imagine Naaman's clenched jaw and the sound of his horse taking off as he digs his heels (or spurs if he was from Texas) into the horse's sides. I wonder how long Naaman rode before his servants got the courage to approach him, to encourage him. "Naaman, maybe you were expecting to have healing come in some big, mighty way. Maybe, since this small thing the prophet is asking you to do wouldn't be too bad to do, you could try it. Maybe? Naaman?"

I wonder how long Naaman sat there pondering before he tasted the bile of swallowed pride and turned his horse around. I wonder how many of his army and servant men stood around him as he stripped down to his Skivvies and stepped into the Jordan waters. I wonder if he had someone counting out loud as he dipped his head under.

One . . . he dips again.

Two . . . and again.

Three . . . and again.

Four . . .

Like a bobber being pulled under again and again by the tension of a spinning rod and a caught fish, Naaman dips under the water until finally, *seven*! He is done. The result? "And his flesh was restored and became clean like that of a young boy" (2 Kings 5:14 NIV).

I wonder if each dip brought more restoration, and those on the banks of the Jordan watched the healing occur a little at a time. Or if after the seventh dip, the healing finally occurred. I wonder what it was like for Naaman to look down at his arms and his legs and see transformed flesh, smooth and free from the monstrous disease that, by attacking his skin, had for so many years ravaged his soul. I wonder if he cried. Or if he just stood there in silence, unable to speak. I wonder what stepping out of the water onto the shore was like as he looked at the men before him. I wonder how his voice sounded and if he had to choke out the words "thank you" to the servants who had turned his prideful heart around.

I wonder if every day for the rest of his life he looked back on that one day, realizing how close he had come to missing the miracle because of his pride.

I wonder if, in my twenties, I missed out on the opportunity for healing because I wanted a private, big, miraculous, Red-Sea-splitting, instantaneous miracle. God had something different in mind, something that would bring the darkest part of me out into the light. The most broken part of me that needed healing wasn't my sexuality. It was my pride. Drawing me into a healing opportunity for one, he could address the other.

I sensed that God's next step for me was an opportunity to step into the waters of humility in which he wanted to heal me. The process would be slower, brighter, and definitely more public. Others would be standing on the shore watching, possibly counting, waiting . . . to see a miracle.

The opportunity came packaged as an eight-week class on relational and sexual brokenness that was being held at church. The three heroes of faith who had stood on stage had talked about it. God was opening the door for me to take the class. This wasn't a command or demand. He was inviting. He was willing and able and was simply asking, was I?

Donald Miller, in *Scary Close*, quotes someone who told him, "We will never feel loved until we drop the act, until we're willing to show our true selves to the people around us."[3] Signing up for this class was the first step for me to own in a very public way that something just might be really off in me. I had wires crossed that needed uncrossing. Inside my heart and my soul there was a leprous disease that needed healing. There was something weak or broken in me. If you remember, that wasn't allowed. I was still a protector and a performer. I wasn't allowed to be weak or diseased. I still was moving through life with "pretty is as pretty does" and "please give me praise" fueling my every move.

Yet the invitation sat there staring at me, taunting me to attend this class. It would silently stare me down, asking me to admit that I was a broken, hot mess, and, yes, weak. My pride hated it.

This reminds me, may I share my favorite story on pride? It's found in John 8.

Imagine with me a woman dragged into the temple. She is thrown, crying, into the middle of a circle. The men who brought her are holding rocks in their hands as they stand all around. They yell. Others begin to yell with them. Children look on, learning this is what happens to someone who "sins."

She stands there, head down, defeated, humiliated, weak, wanting something, anything to cover her shame. The yells seem to get louder, until she hears the mob quiet down as an angry older man loudly questions another man inside the circle. This younger man is different from all the other men she's known before. His eyes . . . not that she dares more than a quick glance. She is too ashamed and afraid to look up. After all, she knows the truth. She is guilty. She knows what she deserves.

Oddly, despite the question asked across the circle, the silence continues. Jesus, the one questioned, hasn't answered. The woman bravely peeks up and is startled because Jesus is near her, bent down, drawing something with his fingers on the ground. She feels the wind shift as he stands. Gently, yet firmly, he speaks to the angry man and the crowd of men who still hold their rocks. "Let any one of you who is without sin be the first to throw a stone at her" (John 8:7 NIV).

Silence echoes in response as Jesus stoops down again . . . still near her. He is close enough to her to be hit by a stone. The reality of this shakes her reality. *What is this man doing?* her mind screams, only to be silenced by the sound of one of the rocks hitting the ground, but it's not near her . . . or him. The sound comes from the outer circle of men.

Another thud sounds a little farther off, then another and another, as rock after rock is dropped.

An eerie silence fills the temple. Her accusers are gone. Only Jesus, next to her, remains. She bravely glances at him, still drawing on the ground. She panics, searching frantically as to what to do. He seems focused as he continues to draw.

As if on cue, Jesus stands and calmly looks at her. Her tense, self-protective stance begins to soften as she finally braves her fear enough to make eye contact with him and sees the kindness in his eyes.

His eyes . . . it's impossible to describe them with words. They are so gentle, so kind. She just stands there, absorbing soundless words that stream from his eyes.

He asks, "Where are they? Has no one condemned you?" (John 8:10 NIV).

She glances down as the tears collect on her bare, dirty feet. "No one, Lord" (John 8:11), she quietly replies.

He pauses and waits to respond. He wants her to see his eyes again. She steadies herself enough to glance up.

Words follow what has already been spoken into her soul. "Neither do I. Go and sin no more" (John 8:11 NLT).

Circle of Judgment

I wonder, what do you really know of this story? You might have read it a hundred times before, or maybe this is the first time you've experienced the story of the woman caught in adultery.

It's easily my favorite story in the Bible, because I know what it's like to be in the middle of the circle. I know what it's like to sit in a crowd of judgment, with others poised and ready and many standing all around—hunters on the hunt. Standing there, surrounding another helpless prey.

That's what it has felt like at times, being gay, with the world standing around . . . Wait. No, change that to the church standing around, rocks in hand, like hunters on the hunt with a trapped and encircled new prey. And you stand there sinking in the sands of shame, living a life you still can't believe you're living and for which you're about to be stoned.

Maybe that doesn't resonate. Maybe you're not gay. But you're you, and you're not perfect. You've felt the circle of condemnation when, at one time, you too were the prey of the world or the church. Maybe you cheated or lied or drank too much, again. Maybe you were condemned because of your weight or hair, your loudness or quietness, that temper you still can't control, or the porn you can't seem not to watch. Maybe you were condemned because you're not more like your sibling or because you like Jesus too much and need to settle down.

Yet what do we see Jesus do?

He enters into the drama of the circle where she is. He doesn't stand above her. He is near her, with her. He risks for her. He gets dirty in the dirt for her. He waits and waits some more until she is ready to face the truth.

Notice what he doesn't do. He doesn't make her look at him. He doesn't make her listen. He simply draws near and waits.

I wonder, isn't this where the miracle of transformation begins—in the dirt of our lives, in the mess of our sin, in the one area of our lives we'd most like to hide?

Jesus's desire is to come into *that* circle and face *those* people about *that* issue. He waits to come and be with us and have the opportunity to speak to us. What if he did?

Pause before you answer that, so I can have you answer something else.

Wouldn't the magical dust experience we secretly hope for ruin that? If I could pray a formula prayer or wave some magic wand and instantly have what I want, wouldn't I miss the real miracle—that I was loved enough that Jesus would even join me in my mess?

Isn't that the real miracle? At my worst, Jesus wants to enter in so he can love me the most.

I wonder if that's why he passed by the blind men the first time. Was it so they could develop more faith, more hunger, more perseverance so that by the time they reached him, he could love on them more in a personal, intimate setting? I wonder if that's why he didn't answer my prayer for healing in my twenties. He wanted more personal, more intimate. Me? I wanted drive-thru, give-it-to-me-quick, silver-bullet-style healing.

Throwing Stones

Look back with me at the story of the woman caught in adultery. Do you notice something else? It's something I've not noticed until now: *transformation happens only after the rocks of condemnation get dropped.*

It's a powerful reality to ponder, isn't it? I often wonder about the older man who first dropped his stone. I wonder what his sin was. What memory, do you think, came flooding back in, uninvited? I wonder if he felt shame as his fingers relaxed and surrendered the rock to gravity's natural force. I hope not. Shame is Satan's white straitjacket that no one should have to wear.

I wonder what would happen if we all did this. What if we all dropped our rocks? What if I chose to drop my rocks of judgment against you, and you chose to drop yours against me? Wouldn't that help things?

It's hard, I know. We hold the rocks in our hands for a reason. Who's being judged inside your circle while you stand on the outer circle poised to throw your rock? Gay people? Straight people? Religious people? Muslim people? Darker people? Whiter people? Your sister? Your mother? Your ex? Democrats? Conservatives? Environmentalists? Carnivores? Those who don't recycle? Your neighbor and his pooping dog? Your spouse? Your child who can't seem to get it right?

And what is your stone of choice? What do you most like to throw? Your words? Your glances? The rolling of your eyes that you perfected in eighth grade? Your stone-cold silence? Your fist? What would it feel like to put that down? How would that free you, and how would it free them? What does hating them so much give you? Power? Control? A pedestal to stand on? What would it take for you to step off that pedestal of power and let that rock go? Jesus is whispering to you, "The sinless one among you, go first: throw the stone."

Dropping your rock will be hard, yes, but if the Pharisees could do it, I know you can too. It will be worth it. And perhaps, like me, it will prepare you to drop the rock against the one you're angriest at. Oh yes, there's a more challenging circle I stand on the edge of. In the center of this circle is Jesus. Everything in me wants to throw that stone at him

for the dreams he never fulfilled,

for the ones he let shatter,

for the wounds he let happen,

for who he claims to be and who he seems to be, and

because in my life, those two often have been quite different.

As I stand in all my glory on the outside of the circle, I know this one thing: it's either him or me.

The Other Me

If I am honest, I have to admit that I like the power of standing in my judgmental place holding my rock. It feels good. He no longer gets to judge me. After all, the version of me who holds the rock in my hand is strong, opinionated, knows how to get things done. She knows how things should be.

Jesus is in the center of the circle, protecting, valuing, loving, next to a crumpled piece of nothing curled up on the ground. I shift a little to catch a glimpse of who it is. The worthless mess too weak to stand lying next to him in the dirt is *me*. It's the other me, the me I don't let anyone see. Why would I? She's weak, insecure, needy, and I hate her. I want her dead. Seriously, I want her dead.

Jesus stoops next to that aching soul that desperately needs to be loved and lifted up. His face is sad, because he feels the pain of the wounded me. He is waiting, wanting to love me and hold me, desiring to provide for me and protect me.

The pride-filled me stands strong on the outer circle with rock in hand, waiting, watching, calculating, making sure no one sees the inner me. Pride-filled me couldn't handle that—the weak and wounded being seen.

I must maintain my image. Isn't that the kicker? I carry and throw rocks to protect my image. I easily could spend the rest of my life throwing rocks, all to maintain my precious, whatever-you-do-don't-tarnish-it image.

Don't we all do it though? Don't we throw rocks at the people who threaten to tarnish our image? Their very presence threatens us. Not only that, but, like the Pharisees, we throw rocks at others to *improve* our image. Destroying their image improves mine. Their badness shines light on my goodness, and I like the spotlight.

I don't just throw rocks at others. Oh no, that's not enough. The greatest threat to my precious image is that weakling inside the inner circle whom I don't want anyone to see—me. I save the biggest rock for me. In fact, I'd pick up a boulder to use on me if my biceps were big enough. I don't like to work that hard in the gym, so a decent-sized rock will have to do. Luckily, it's enough, because I'm weak. The me who sits inside the circle of pain stays silent as the me on the outside threatens with the rock I hold overhead.

Let me ask you: Do you want to be transformed? I said *transformed*, not better or different. To be transformed involves a completely different conversation with a completely different outcome. The work, well, it occurs in a completely different location, and the work is hard . . . very, very hard.

Behavioral Management

To be made better or different occurs outside the circle. The type of work that occurs there is called behavioral management. Have you heard of it? This is where I roll up my sleeves and get to work. I work on controlling my behavior and on managing my sins. I work on not committing them. I work on being nicer—especially while driving in rush-hour traffic or on Monday mornings before I've had my coffee. I try to manage my behavior and, in doing so, guess what else I manage?

Bingo! You're right! I manage my image! When I'm able to manage my behavior, I'm able to manage my image, and who doesn't want a better image? Sign me up for that!

Most people do want to be better. They want to cuss less, give more, have an easier time saying no to that thing they struggle to say no to. They'd like to be a little more consistent, a little more disciplined, and a little more whole. Those would be things worth working for. That's doable work, and we like doable, don't we? A little nip here, a little tuck there. No problem.

To be *transformed* is an entirely different story. That's inner-circle work that can be done only inside the circle of pain. But who wants to go there? Let's keep that door closed and locked. After all, it's been closed for a reason, hasn't it? The key to that door was thrown away years ago, and for good reason, right? The last time that door was opened there was pain, a lot of it. So let's build a wall around that door. No one gets in there: not you, not me. Jesus? Not him either.

Instead, we just settle for better and skip that transformation stuff. We'll save that for the extremists and socially awkward. They can take care of it.

Let's Get Real

The reality, friend, is that the only thing that has brought transformation in my life is opening the door to the inner circle, when I quit pretending I wasn't a hot mess in need of a real hug and a long shower. I had to let Jesus into the inner circle and give him permission to touch the pain in order for me to feel his promises—the promise of his love, the promise of his protection, the promise of his provision.

Notice what I didn't say. I didn't say he had to touch the pain for me to *hear* his promise. I'd heard the words before. I didn't need to hear them again. What I needed was to *feel* his love. I needed to *feel* his protection. I needed to *feel* his provision. But I couldn't do that when the real part of me wasn't allowed to *feel* at all. That cord was severed a long time ago, and I was operating off only a small portion of my heart. Behavior management and a little bit better was just going to have to do.

There's only one problem. Jesus doesn't do behavior management. He'd rather set us free. He wants us, like the adulterous woman, to experience love and go forward in our lives free. Free from pain, shame, and sin. As Paul reminded the Galatians, "It is for freedom that Christ has set us free" (Gal. 5:1 NIV).

The chains of slavery pull us backward because most of the time we don't really want transformation and freedom. We want to stay the same. Same is safe. Same is easy. Same is predictable. I know how to navigate and control "same," because I take it and live it everywhere I go.

Isn't who I am now good enough? Isn't that enough? When is it enough? When I sin less and show up more like Mother Teresa? Can't I be done transforming? Because I want to be done; I so badly want to be done. But I am not done, am I? Sigh. No. Sigh.

Neither are you, and neither is Jesus. He's not done until we are free. And we aren't even close to free. We live enslaved to the prideful voice that tells us to self-protect and self-provide in order to keep the wounded part of us silent. We do and act and perform so that it won't be seen. We spend our lives feeding our faces and starving our souls.

We think it's better than the alternative, which is facing the pain, the pain that lies inside the circle. The weak one lying there? She holds it. She carries it. I make her hide it inside her soul. Anytime she tries to make a sound or cry for help, I raise my rock high in the air and I threaten. She'd better shut up. I don't want her to be seen.

But Jesus won't let the past go. He just won't leave it alone. I get so mad at him, because I want it to be left alone. I don't want to go back to those memories. I don't want to revisit that pain. If I have to feel the flames of hell as Jesus rescues me, why would I want heaven? I don't want to transform that badly. Just a little better, a little different will do. But I see his eyes, and I know it's a lie. A little won't do.

I pray as you read this that you will stop and look at him too and will see that, for you, a little just won't do either. He wants to enter into your inner circle, where the worst of you lies—the wounded one, the part you've already judged as worthless. Isn't that what happened to the adulterous woman? The Pharisees threw her inside the circle and, from their lofty positions, slammed the gavel down and judged her *worthless*. Isn't this what Christians have done to homosexuals for years?

But Jesus saw her. He went to her, stayed by her. With his eyes, with his mercy, with his presence, with his grace, he said, "They are wrong. You are worthy."

That, my friend, is the miracle moment when we transform. In that moment, when the worst of us sees the best of him, we change—*forever.*

Swimming with Sharks

It happened for me on December 6, 2009.

I had resigned to signing up for that eight-week class, which ended up being an eight-week torture session that wounded my pride. I will confess, I signed up only because God asked me to, and I was still living in the year of "I will do whatever you ask me to." This brings up a necessary topic on the way of work—obedience.

It takes work to be obedient. There are a hundred voices giving you a thousand reasons not to do the one thing you are being asked to do that you don't want to do. It's work to move that foot forward, when all you want to do is step backward.

That class was a battle for obedience, a battle that took some time to win. I went the first couple of weeks and *hated* it. I hated sitting in a group with strangers talking about stuff I didn't want to talk about to my plants, who know how to keep a secret, let alone strangers in a group. Mostly I just stared and sat silently, wondering how I had gotten suckered into going and how mean everyone looked.

The middle weeks I went backward, which is a frequent occurrence for anyone God is calling forward. Satan will wave something shiny behind you and tempt you to step back toward it. Step back I did. The old life knocked, and I ran to get the door. When I say it knocked, it was more likely the sound of my pounding heart at the unknown that God was calling me to. I tried to go back to old friendships, old relationships, anything to make me feel something other than fear and anxiety. That's what good codependents know how to do best. We use someone else to feed our souls all from a place of selfish desires. I felt God trying to call me forward into the new and unknown, so I raced back to the comfortable and controllable. In those three weeks, I deeply wounded the people from my past I tried to use. I fell for the mirage of life-giving water that turned out to be only sand.

I share this to say, if God is calling you forward into healing and the work of transformation, be brave. Keep stepping forward. If while reading this you realize your last step was placed behind you, it's okay. Three weeks, three months, or three years of back stepping doesn't matter. Simply pause, give yourself grace, and start moving forward again.

For me, after eating sand for three or four weeks, I was back in class for week seven and then the last class on December 6.

If you've been to a Celebrate Recovery or an AA-style group, you know the format: large-group, coed teaching session. Break up into gender-specific small groups for prayer and sharing. Ugh.

Funny thing about that last Sunday class, December 6 of '09. That week I was the only female who showed up. Yep, the *only* girl.

Imagine walking from one building, after the large-group teaching time, to another building across church property for small-group time. *Now* imagine you're the only girl making this walk—and four female leaders are walking behind you.

I felt like a minnow about to be eaten by piranhas, and they might as well have been. They were women who could chew you up and spit you out without blinking. Do you know women like these? Women who can cut through the meaty BS you are serving with a dull plastic spoon? Women who know you're a fake and are willing to call you on it? Women who see what you don't want anyone to see because they have some kind of spiritual sonar that sniffs out struggle and sin? Oh yes. They were four of *those* kinds of women. Women who might as well have had a headset on with a direct line from God, who is sharing everything you've done and everything he knows. And if you're not very familiar with God, he knows a lot.

While my feet were walking, my mind was running the numbers:

1 minnow

4 sharks (yes, they grew in scariness as we walked)

60 minutes

1:4 x 60 minutes

I was toast. Like Jack Bauer scanning for a way out of a burning building, I began calculating whether I could outrun them. I am still not sure how I made it to the other building rather than sprinting to my car and making a *Fast and Furious* dash out of the parking lot. I made it to a rocking chair in the nursing mothers' room in which we met.

The good news, I found out as we all got nestled in our chairs, was that they weren't going to ask me any questions. Nice. I didn't want to talk. The bad news was that they were just going to pray. Seriously? For an hour? What kind of torture was this? I'd rather be eaten alive than prayed to death.

There I was, dying one affirming prayer at a time. But in the middle of one of those prayers, something happened. I was sitting calmly, quietly minding my own business (which means I was externally calm, eyes closed, acting like I was praying too, but internally freaking out). The next thing I heard was one of the ninja ladies asking Jesus to show himself to me, to let me see him sitting next to me or standing out in the hall.

This is a bizarre request, I thought. You don't just "see" Jesus.

As my mind was arguing this known fact, I found myself peeking around to see if he was there. I was peeking with my eyes closed. I know, it doesn't make sense, but stay with me because, as my search continued, the woman praying said, "O, Jesus, if you're standing in the doorway . . ."

Bam! If I didn't see Jesus right then standing in the doorway, leaning against the door frame, looking at me, with a sadness I can't begin to describe.

It was simply crushing. His eyes, the love he had for me, and yet the utter sadness he was carrying because I wouldn't let him close. It was instantly clear that he wanted inside the inner circle to love on the real me, the pain-filled mess who seemed worthless and unlovable. He wanted to love that me.

But Now I See

Yes, I saw Jesus. Not in the way I can see the red couch I am sitting on or the fireplace in front of me. My eyes were closed the entire time, and the door to the room was closed.

How could I see Jesus standing in a closed doorway with my eyes shut? I don't know. I just saw him. You might call it a vision. You might call it something else. Me? I just call it real, because it was. My life has been completely different ever since. That's what happens when the worst of us encounters the best of him. We are transformed.

Unveiled

What I couldn't explain then I understand now through Paul's words: "And we all, with unveiled face, beholding the glory of the Lord, are being transformed into the same image from one degree of glory to another" (2 Cor. 3:18).

Lots of pieces make up this puzzle of a verse, so let's look at each piece separately so that it makes more sense.

"And we all, with unveiled face"

The "we all" Paul refers to here is not only the church in Corinth but also those of us who are Christ-followers now. Earlier in the second chapter, Paul explained the concept of the veil and how, when a person's heart is hardened toward God, it's as if she is wearing a veil and is unable to clearly see and that only through

Christ is this veil taken away, that only through Christ can someone be free and really see.

"beholding the glory of the Lord"

If you dive into the Greek, the word for this phrase is *katoptrizō*, translated as "beholding as in a mirror," which sounds kind of funny to me. The word *seeing* can be used as a substitute if it helps. Yet, "seeing as in a mirror" still sounds kind of funny, doesn't it?

Think about the last time you looked in a mirror. Was it the last time you went to the bathroom? Were you washing your hands and then sucking in, flexing, or rearranging whatever needed to be rearranged so you were able to accept the image that stared back? Admit it. You flexed something, didn't you? (It's okay, I did too!)

Imagine, though, if when you glanced in the mirror, what looked back wasn't you but Jesus. How would that change you? What would you try to shift or flex or fix then? Funny thing to consider, isn't it? Think about how often you look in a mirror. Five times a day? Ten? Twenty-plus times a day?

"are being transformed into the same image from one degree of glory to another."

What does Paul say when who we see is Jesus? What happens when we behold or see "the glory of the Lord"?

What happens? We transform. What do you notice about this transformation? It's from what to what? Yep, it's from one degree of glory to another.

Again, how does that transformation happen? When we are looking at whom? *Jesus.* When we look at Jesus, we become like Jesus.

Behold Him

To behold Jesus is to see Jesus. It's the *real* you seeing the *real* him. On that day, in that rocking chair, I was able to behold Jesus beholding me, to see him leaning against the door frame of the nursing mothers' room, so willing, so able. All he wanted to do was to come closer, to sit by me, to be with me.

Me. The girl who,

thought she wasn't worth fighting for,
had to keep it all together,
had to perform,
had to protect.

He was seeing *me* for the real *me*, not the act or the show I put on for others. He didn't have a need. He just wanted me. He wanted me to know I was loved. As. I. Was.

He saw that so much of what I had done or who I was trying to be was out of a need for love. And here he was, offering more of it than I could handle. Literally, in that moment, I asked him to stay there by the door. I couldn't handle him coming any closer. The amount of love he was offering, if he came closer, was just too much.

The prayer time wrapped up, and I was released from the shark tank where the prayer sharks had been praying. Dazed and overwhelmed, I walked into our Sunday evening service, which started conveniently right after the class. I sat in the back and during worship, while everyone else stood, singing, I crumpled over, my head in my hands and my hands on my knees, curled up in a ball so no one could see the flood of tears. As they streamed from my closed eyes, I saw him again. Still standing in that same doorway, waiting. He was letting me know I had a choice. Do I let him come closer? Do I accept the overwhelming love he is offering?

Close to hyperventilating from the uncontrollable sobs, I nodded at him, yes. He could come.

It's unclear what happened after I said yes. He stepped toward me and the vision ended. In that moment, I felt, I experienced, *love*.

So much so, that on December 7, 2009, I woke up not knowing what to do with my life. I remember coming out of my bedroom, staring at my dogs, then scanning my living room, frozen. I didn't know what to do. I literally didn't think I needed to go to work that day. There was no point. Everything I had used work for I had received one hundred times over the night before. My entire life prior to that moment had been filled with attempts to feel loved and be loved, or to earn love or keep love. Every waking second had been devoted to that one pursuit.

In that instant, the night before, I experienced it. *Love.* There was nothing left in life that I needed to pursue. I felt complete.

So why was December 6 so transformative? I'd heard I was loved a thousand times from friends and family. I'd heard God loves me a thousand times more. What was so different this time?

In looking back at the circles, I find the answer. When the pride-filled, protector, outer-circle version of me got the information that I was loved by God, nothing really happened. After all, pride doesn't need love from Jesus or others because it is too busy loving, worshiping, and protecting itself. But in that moment, on that Sunday, at about 4:30 in the afternoon, I was undone. The inner-circle me was seen and touched, forever changed, as I saw I was actually *loved*.

I beheld him beholding me.

This change requires you to travel down the way of work. It takes work to get pride out of the way. It takes work to stop listening to lies. It takes work to stop looking at God and the world through a small-lens, self-centered, self-protective perspective. It's simply easier to behold what I want, when I want, the way I want—having things my way.

We are a culture of disruptions and distractions. We like the disruption of the message light that blinks on our smartphones. We like the distractions of the hashtags and the newsfeeds. We love the likes we get from the highlight reel we post of our Snapchat, Facebook-frenzied lives and the instantaneous thumbs-up that we recieve.

Pride, camped out on the outer circle, loves these. We get to feel important, needed, successful, and in the know. We love to be in the know. We understand that FOMO (fear of missing out) is a real disease. We sit and stare for hours at illuminated screens. Pride likes to glance around, noticing who is noticing us. Isn't it interesting?

We become *what we behold*. It's true, which leaves me wondering, What might life be like if we changed what we behold? My realization? *Hope* happens when we change our view.

A Central Focus

If you are like me, the number one thing I stare at most is myself.

I am constantly looking at me to see how I am measuring up, to see how I am feeling, to see what I want to do, to see how I am going to solve that problem so I can congratulate myself on coming through or beat myself up for being such a failure. What I behold most, if I am honest, is me. My pride is always looking out for me.

Isn't that the real issue—that as I stand proudly on the outer circle, I spend every moment of every day looking at me? When I go to work, I'm looking at and thinking about me. When I hang out, I am looking at and thinking about me. When I am at church, yes, even church, my prideful self dresses up and plays the part so you too will look at and think about me.

I'm obsessed with me.

In a culture in which we obsess over what we possess, I don't even notice Jesus. But that's on purpose, of course. In our rock-holding and outer-circle standing, we spend our time looking away from Jesus to the things we want. Our pride has us glancing at everyone and everything in comparison to see what we can puff up our chests over, or sulk and strategize over how to change. Our prideful self doesn't need to look inside that circle at Jesus for help. We got it.

We sure can't look inside that circle at what's lying next to Jesus. Our weak and wounded self, lying there in the circle of pain, is safely secure beneath the blanket of shame we like to hide under.

We dare not have that part of us glance up at him. No, no, that level of vulnerability will never do.

But what if we were that brave? Brave enough to be vulnerable. Brave enough to let the worst of us glance up and behold the best of him. I say we have to be. To walk the way of hope, it's required. I must be vulnerable, yes, vulnerable. Ugh.

Ugh to the ickiness of the word. It sounds slimy. Have you ever looked up the definition of *vulnerable*? It's as awful as it sounds: "capable of or susceptible to being wounded or hurt, as by a weapon."[4]

Thanks but no thanks, right? Prideful protector is stationed on the outer circle for a reason. Give me one more day of self-protection, please! After all, who wants to be susceptible to being wounded again, especially by God.

What if you are wrong? What if he is safe and good and wants you to see him, *really* see him? Isn't it worth being brave and vulnerable to give him a chance, to uncover your face and let him see you and, most importantly, be able to see him?

This is your story, and your story isn't over. I want to encourage you to push pride aside and give Jesus a chance to behold you. But I warn you, be careful. When you behold him, it will undo you. Change you. You will never be the same. And it will challenge what you've built your life upon. It will require you to start on a new area of work—your beliefs.

9

The Way of *More* Work

Isn't it funny how we live inside the lies we believe?

A. S. King[1]

We're going to have to let truth scream louder to our souls than the lies that have infected us.

Beth Moore[2]

Isn't strength the ability to renounce every lie in your heart?

Bisco Hatori[3]

Like the title of this chapter? Me neither.

If you're like me, the last thing you want in life is more work. But if you want the real version of my story, that's what this journey has been—*The Way of* More *Work*.

A Journey

If we review Paul's words from 2 Corinthians 3:18, we will see an important piece of the puzzle that explains why transformation involves *more* work: "And we all, with unveiled face, beholding the glory of the Lord, are being transformed into the same image from *one degree of glory to another*" (emphasis added).

Transformation happens, one degree at a time.

In our fast-food, give-it-to-me-now, Amazon-delivery-in-an-hour culture, *one degree at a time* doesn't seem very fast. Especially when you are trying to turn your life around. I often encounter people who think that my journey has been one in which God sprinkled magical fairy dust on me and instantly I was healed, transformed, and made straight. While I do believe God does sometimes heal people in powerful, miraculous moments, my journey has been just that, a journey, taken one *slow*, painful step at a time.

That's not very inspiring, perhaps, but truth can be the most inspirational thing there is. When traveling down the way of hope, truth is a vital necessity empowering you to keep moving forward, even if the journey takes longer than you'd like.

Even though my encounter with radical love on December 6 did more for my heart than I can put into words, it was only the beginning. Like Naaman at the river, I needed a few more dips for real healing to occur.

My dips weren't into a creek or a river. The dips I needed were into the pool of truth, as my life had been muddied and caked with lies. Yes, lies, lies, lies. Lies woven into my heart, anchored deep in wounds, locked safely in rooms, with keys that I couldn't seem to find. But seeing Jesus on that Sunday afternoon started unlocking doors for me. A lie was revealed that I had been believing: *God doesn't care about me.*

On that Sunday afternoon, beholding Jesus, I clearly saw the truth, leaning against the door frame. He was there. He cared.

What I was beholding didn't match up with what I had been believing. I had a choice. Do I let what I am beholding change what I have been believing? Do I renounce the lie that God doesn't care about me?

This is where the *more* work comes in. On the journey of transformation, I had to change not only what I was beholding or seeing but also what I believed.

In my life, the space in my vault that hadn't been taken up with secrets had been filled with lies. It was filled with lies about God, lies about myself, lies about men, and lies about women. When looking at the process of transformation in myself, I see it happened according to Paul's words in Romans: "Do not conform to the pattern of this world, but be transformed by the renewing of your mind. Then you will be able to test and approve what God's will is—his good, pleasing and perfect will" (12:2 NIV).

Transformation occurred only as I let my mind be renewed. The lies I was carrying around behind locked doors had to be let out, looked at, and renounced—one by one.

If my mind stored the lie, there was usually a related wound in my heart. To address the lie, I had to let God address the wound it was embedded in, and vice versa.

God started unlocking doors so that lies and wounds could be revealed. All these doors were unlocked through opportunities that required me to strip down to my Skivvies like Naaman (so to speak) and be emotionally naked in front of people. Over the past seven years, God has asked me to do things that have stripped me of my pride and made visible to all (or at least all who might be present) that weak, wounded little girl whom I made lie there, hidden under a blanket of shame inside the inner circle. She was the one wounded. She was the one believing the lies.

Torture Weekend

One of the next things God asked me to do after the class ended was to attend a women's weekend retreat. Some of you just cringed along with me. Thank you for feeling my pain. Isn't that a literal nightmare for someone with zero security in her femininity? (Yea, God . . . that's a great idea. I'd love to spend a weekend with women completely different from me. I'd love to give a room full of women the whole weekend to judge me. Yes, I'd love for the weekend's topic to be on identity. I'd love to dive into that with women who will reject me. That'd be just *super*! Great idea! So glad you suggested it!)

But I went. It's the way of *more* work. *More* obedience is *more* work. It's prying your body off the couch, which feels like life, and getting in the car and driving to an event that feels likes death. It's facing the possibility of rejection by others when you get there. It's slipping into the bathroom multiple times throughout the first night because you don't know how to stay in the room and survive normal "female" conversation. Even though you've done it before in your women's small group, the fact that it's a four-day weekend retreat changes all the rules. You are rooming with someone you don't know, and you don't know if you will have to do the dreaded "bed sharing," which triggers all your fears, especially if your previous recreational lifestyle choices should come out at some point. Believe me, at a Christian women's weekend event like that, you'd rather be the one known for snoring or wetting the bed than being gay.

But I survived. More than that, I learned that I was wrong. The lies that I believed about myself and other women weren't true. Following are a list of the lies that the weekend (as well as other scary weekends, small groups, trips, outings, coffees, and dinners over the past seven years) forced me to face and address:

I'm too different.

Truth: I'm not that different. Some of the same insecurities, fears, shame, guilt, and pain I've struggled with are common for women of all types. They've just packaged them differently because of the lies they've believed.

Women are scared and won't be friends with me because of my past.

Truth: God has gifted women to see past the mud to the masterpiece underneath; hiding behind judgment isn't fair to them or to me.

I can't trust other women.

Truth: I can trust God enough to protect me as I learn which women are trustworthy enough to be called friends.

I must remain closed off emotionally, physically, and spiritually to protect them and me.

Truth: It's not *my* job to protect myself. It's God's job. I can trust the Holy Spirit to speak to me if there is a woman I am encountering with which good boundaries are needed, even if that woman is me.

Truth: I *need* godly women in my life to be God's presence and hands of comfort to me. I need nurturing hugs and nurturing words spoken to me. I need godly women fighting for me in prayer.

It's safer to be masculine than feminine.

Truth: All women have differing levels of femininity and masculinity. We *can* be strong and tender at the same time. If I live only from a place of masculinity, I am presenting a false self and denying the tender, feminine side inherent in me. It's unsafe to live from this place of complete masculinity; by doing so, the real me can never be loved because it's never given a chance to be seen.

I'm the only woman who feels like this.

Truth: Women of all shapes, sizes, likes, and dislikes feel the same way I do. We *all* want to be loved, to be beautiful to someone, to feel worthy and be valued. We want to feel that who we are is enough.

Spending the weekend with those women and taking a risk at being seen as I was gave me the opportunity to see them as they really were. It allowed me to see how I was hiding behind the judgments and fears I held against them. It allowed me to once again uncross my self-protective arms and open my heart and give them the opportunity to speak life and truth into me. The weekend proved to be another necessary dip into the pool of truth's healing waters.

The Big Ask

I will warn you that this next story is a bit painful for me to tell. At times, when walking away from the same-sex lifestyle, I thought I was going to lose my mind. The pain of breaking the chains of codependency would overwhelm me. There was even a span of time from October to December of '09 that, regardless of where you ran into me, I'd have headphones on listening to either worship music or a sermon on podcast. The thoughts racing through my head trying to talk me back into my old life were so loud. Those moments were tough. Working through my gender/sexuality issues was tough.

Looking back, one of the *toughest* things God asked me to do to unlock some of the lies I was believing had nothing to do with my sexuality . . . not a thing. Yet it has brought healing to my identity and sexuality in a way I find difficult to describe.

The ask, you ask? It came when God asked me to give up my drug of choice—work. Yes, in December of '09, God asked me to quit teaching and coaching.

It happened late one night, over Christmas break, when I was just wasting time on the computer seeing if any Christian bands were coming into town. The thought was subtle at first, and then it became a stronger prompting. I thought that God wanted me to quit my job and go overseas as a missionary. This was rather comical at first; I was sure I was hearing him wrong. After all, I was still in my first year of my dream coaching job at a great school and had bought my first house a few months before. So his timing was, well, inconvenient for my plans. Surely, he understood. After all, I was doing a good thing! I was pouring into kids. I was not only going to church but also serving on the greeting team at church. I handed out the programs. I helped pass the offering buckets from time to time. I was even starting to talk to kids and parents about Jesus. I was being missional. Right?

I knew I could do a little more. Things didn't have to get as drastic as me quitting my job and moving across the world. I had nephews and dogs, for goodness' sake! Who would help take care of them?

Clearly, he would. I wasn't needed for that. I simply was supposed to trust, to obey. I was supposed to resign my job and finish out the school year. Then pursue going overseas—far, far away. Alone.

I'd love to tell you that after the prompting, the argument between God and me lasted about two hours or even two weeks. But my faith at that time (and sometimes still now) was often weak due to self-centeredness and fear. Instead, I argued for two months, trying to convince him of all the reasons I shouldn't resign and go. After all, I wasn't in the lifestyle anymore, though I wasn't that far out of it either.

Finally, I saw he was serious, and I somehow surrendered. I began making emotional plans to leave. Telling a few people here and a few more there, trying to rally support to do the big deed he was asking—to resign my job.

I am not sure I can put into words the pain of that day, walking into the principal's office and laying my resignation letter on her desk. The look of shock on her face; she didn't understand. My words of explanation that "I feel like God is asking me to do this" felt hollow and weak. But the pain of that day was *nothing* compared to the pain of walking into the gym a few weeks later to tell the amazing young ladies I had the honor of coaching that I wouldn't be back. The trust and belief in themselves that we had worked so hard to build seemed to fracture and scatter on the floor in an instant. Maybe it wasn't their feelings but mine, as I left a piece of my heart on that gym floor that day.

Likely some of you reading this don't get it. God's never asked you to leave something you've loved that deeply. You've never listened closely enough for fear he might ask. Others of you do get the tears that are streaming down my face right now. God asked you to leave something or someone, and you know the pain and the reality when all you can do is simply hold on to Jesus's words and promise in Luke 18: "'Truly I tell you,' Jesus said to them, 'no one who has left home or wife or brothers or sisters or parents or children for the sake of the kingdom of God will fail to receive many times as much in this age, and in the age to come eternal life'" (vv. 29–30).

Out of obedience, you let go of that job, thing, relationship, or place you lived, as you grabbed hold of the promise of future blessings in one hand and grabbed Kleenex for the tears and the pain in the other. I get it.

Letting go of what is important to us is hard. But it's possible and sometimes requested. I'd love to tell you the amazing story of what it is like to serve as a full-time missionary overseas. I'd love to share that story, except I haven't lived that story. I never got to go.

After I resigned my job and set out to find a mission agency in obedience to his call, he, well, changed his mind.

I was all set with an acceptance letter to serve overseas, was praying through the team I would join, was starting to begin the process of raising money, and was selling my stuff. Then one morning I got the message that I wasn't supposed to go. I was reading through Ezekiel 3, and suddenly I knew—*I wasn't going.*

I am not sending you to a foreign people whose language you cannot understand. No, I am not sending you to people with strange and difficult speech. If I did, they would listen! But the people of Israel won't listen to you any more than they listen to me! For the whole lot of them are hard-hearted and stubborn. (vv. 5–7 NLT)

For some of you, this sounds strange. How did I know instantly after reading this that God wasn't sending me? It's hard to describe if Scripture hasn't spoken to you yet. Like instantly-jumped-off-the-page, grabbed-you-by-the-shirt-collar, demanded-you-pay-attention-to-a-verse-or-verses kind of speaking to you. If you haven't had one of those moments, keep reading Scripture until it happens. Keep asking the Holy Spirit to make Scripture come alive for you. Most of all, *want* Scripture to speak to you. More than anything else, *want* it that badly. Dive into it with that much hunger. Be open to letting it offend you and say things you don't like. If you don't let Scripture offend you, it can't encourage you. If you won't let Scripture rebuke you, it can't reward you either.

That verse grabbed me by the T-shirt and instantly I knew; I wasn't going. I was staying, to be missional among a people who could understand me but wouldn't want to hear what I had to say. This surprising turn of events left me in a pickle.

What was I supposed to do now, God? The summer was over, and all the school teaching/coaching jobs were gone. What kind of a job was I supposed to get and do now? How would I afford my house, the bills, or fun? What about dog food?

The Space Between

I'd love to type the amazing story of God's next provision, which included an incredible job with ridiculous benefits where I got to do something I loved day in and day out. Unfortunately, it's not that kind of story. Where he led me next wasn't like that. Instead, it was quite the opposite, as he led me into what I now call *the space between*.

It's the liminal space.

Do you know this space or word—liminality? Authors understand liminality well, as great stories see characters navigate the transitional waters between an inciting incident and its resolution. It's the space between the "Uh oh" and the "Whew, it's all okay." The term *liminality* comes from the Latin word *līmen*, meaning "a threshold." As characters in our own faith story, we face the thresholds that God invites us to step over into a space of liminality. It's the space of transition where our normal thinking is challenged, behaviors are exposed, and new perspectives bud and take root. This space is where we are given the opportunity to learn and to grow.

The liminal space is hard. For anything to bud and grow, a seed's shell must be cracked, giving the appearance of chaos instead of calm, disorder instead of order. Unsure footing characterizes this space, as you aren't where you were, but you're not yet where you are going to be, and the temptation to grab on to anything secure abounds. Think Israelites and the wilderness, and you have the perfect picture of liminality. You're not enslaved, but you haven't yet reached the promised land.

In the liminal space, we are given the opportunity to become courageous, valiant heroes of our stories or to turn aside to the villainous shortcuts of the soul. I like how Richard Rohr describes liminality:

> It is when you have left the tried and true, but have not yet been able to replace it with anything else. It is when you are between your old comfort zone and any possible new answer. If you are not trained in how to hold anxiety, how to live with ambiguity, how to entrust and wait, you will run . . . anything to flee this terrible cloud of unknowing.[4]

My old comfort zone of teaching and coaching forever gone, God was calling me into the liminal space of the not yet and the in-between. In this new liminal space, God would test me to see if I would flee toward that "anything" to find escape and meaning amid the internal chaos and confusion this new season would create.

My mentor, pastor, and friend at church connected me to a job at a property management company working in a cubicle typing for eight hours a day doing data entry a blind monkey could do. Yes, you read that right. This freedom-loving, adventure-seeking, don't-make-me-be-still-or-work-indoors girl got to spend forty hours a week in a fluorescently illuminated box, where my job was to be quiet and still, Monday through Friday, from nine to five.

Sit still.
Be quiet.
Look.
Read.
Type.
Repeat.

God had led me to my own personal hell and asked me to make a living there. Dramatic, yes. I truly felt that's what he had done though. I felt betrayed and abandoned in a liminal hellhole, left alone to emotionally die.

This is a funny situation to be in, if it's not you. You'd think a moment of great obedience would instantly be followed by great reward, right? Sometimes the rewards are wrapped in packages we don't want to see. Yes, like spoiled children at Christmas, we miss the new Lego set or the new Barbie we've been given because we are so busy throwing a fit over the pony we think we deserved but didn't get.

Because I had been so sacrificial and obedient in giving up my teaching/coaching job, I felt that—yes, I admit it—God owed me one. A cubicle? Really, God? Did you miss what I just gave up? This is what I am getting in return? A gray, padded prison cell that I am not even allowed to decorate without rules and someone else's approval? How long is this prison sentence? Do I get time off for good behavior?

No was the answer to the request for time off for good behavior and an early release. My prison sentence in that cubicle of torture lasted a year and a half, and I lived every painful day of it. Why would God reward a step of obedience with a job like that?

Now, years later, sitting out here on the deck overlooking the beautiful waters of Cancun as I write, it's clear. That experience was absolutely the most loving thing he could have done for me.

The reason that liminal space of pain was loving? He had to break me of my addiction to a title. Yes, my entire life I had been using my job to define my identity.

When he asked me to give up teaching and coaching to be a missionary, I was trading one cool title for another. People respect teachers and coaches. The new title of missionary came with some status and respect too. But to go from a head coach to no title, no position of importance, well, let's just say that the first two weeks I spent in "the box" (as I called it) I was in a tailspin. I had no clue who I was. I didn't even know how to introduce myself anymore. I truly began having an identity crisis, drowning in the shame of being nothing. I wasn't doing anything for which the world would want to cheer.

If you remember, since I was a young girl, I had a list to check and to keep.

Earn.
Perform.
Protect.
Repeat.

With this new job, there was nothing to earn, no way to perform, and no one to protect. There was definitely no need to repeat. I couldn't earn praise. What I did and the way I did it didn't matter. Not to anyone outside the company and not really even inside the company. I began going through praise and approval withdrawals!

I know. It's embarrassing to read as well as type.

I share this because that year and a half and the way God gently loved me as he broke me in that job was so beautiful. I cried on the way to work nearly every day, surrendering the day and the outcome to him, knowing that he asked me to be there and could release me to go somewhere else whenever he wanted. That time in the box revealed to me the lies that I believed about him and myself, and it forced me to choose what I would believe: the lies I was hearing or the truth spoken in Scripture that he wanted me to believe. The lies:

- I have to perform for people to like me.
- I must *do* to be loved.
- I must be perfect (do/be everything to everyone).
- God doesn't care enough to change my circumstances.
- God doesn't care enough to fulfill my desires.
- God is mean and punishing me.

Retelling this story encourages me and reminds me that there is always hope in the hard places. For those of you who are living through a season that feels as if it is killing you, it may just be the season that's working most to bring you life. Easy to say, I know. It may not seem comforting to know God is allowing this season for a reason. Those comments always sound trite and empty. In the space between, it is easy to see God as either uncaring or not powerful enough to do something about it. If I've learned anything from that season in the box, it is that sometimes he allows us to travel through the challenges to learn the truth about him, his love, and ourselves.

Tell Me the Truth

Isn't that what sets us free? The truth? According to Jesus, it is: "If you abide in my word, you are truly my disciples, and you will know the truth, and the truth will set you free" (John 8:31–32).

Do you see my favorite word there? *Free.* I like to be free. I love freedom. It comes from knowing the truth, not hearing it or quoting it but knowing it down in your core, deep in that inner circle part of you where truth can unlock the door and set the wounded part of your soul free. Freedom happens when truth is allowed in that deep place.

Look with me at the beginning of verse 31 (a truth that was pivotal for me as I navigated through the year-and-a-half confinement in the box): "If you abide in my word." Did you notice it? The *if? If* you abide in my word, *then* you will know the truth. And *then* the truth will set you free.

For those of you who are new to Scripture, it's important to pay attention to if/thens. Sometimes it is easy to quote the *then* part without doing the *more* work the *if* requires. I believe *this if* is one of the most important ones in Scripture. Without the work of abiding in Scripture and holding on to its truths and promises, I wouldn't have made it through that year and a half without taking matters into my own hands—working out my agenda for my life, in my way and in my time, shortcutting the wilderness to make my own promised land.

Staying connected to Scripture helped me to remember the truth of God's character, promises, will, and ways that I needed to learn and trust. His ways are not *my* ways. He knows the plans he has for me. I don't have to know every detail of them. I am supposed to wait upon the Lord. His timing is different from mine, but it is *better* and can be *trusted.* Countless other verses speak to his goodness and desire to direct my path and remind me not to take things into my own hands.

If I could go back, I would ask God if there was another way for me to learn the lessons that I needed to learn. If not, then I would drink from that cup again. The pain of pruning was worth the fruit that it grew in me.

Yes, pruning. It takes *more* work to be still and allow pruning to occur. I believe learning to be still, to wait, to allow the snip here, the trim of lies there, each time beholding a good God and trusting him with the pruning shears, has been what has made all the difference in me, in my healing, in my freedom. Remember, friend, "It is for freedom that Christ has set us free" (Gal. 5:1 NIV).

The process of pruning is painful but not fatal. The liminal space of the box didn't kill me. Every space between has an ending. God set me free from that job and opened the door for me to step into a new role as a personal development coach, which was life-giving and allowed me to see daylight again. Like Jackie Robinson after taking the risk and going on to steal second base, in this new job I had the opportunity to stand up, stretch my legs, and rest, but just for a second. We aren't meant to stand safely on base any more than baseball players. We are meant to live a life of adventure, to check with our base coach and, upon command, take off into the risk and dare the space between.

So it was that God wound up and threw me another new opportunity for growth. This time the challenge went from a short stint in the world of development coaching to no job. Yep, none. Nada. No job and no income whatsoever.

This was the next big ask. I felt God prompting me to quit working altogether. This ask seemed even more ridiculous than the previous one. After all, who quits their job and merely prays for what they need? Yet I felt that was what he was asking me to do. He wanted me to wake up every day and pray for what I needed. Every bill that needed to be paid. Every meal. Simply pray and watch for his provision.

You may be thinking as I did, Why would God want me not to work? How would not working make my gender identity and sexuality issues better? Oh, friend, sit back and listen, 'cause did it ever!

As you've read, one of the ways I have most struggled in life is rooted in the feeling of abandonment caused by my father and stepfather. I believed I had no safe protector to protect me, no provider to provide for me. So it was up to me to protect and provide—me.

God, by asking me to simply pray and wait in faith for provision, opened the wound and illuminated this fear of abandonment and need. God was pressing me to trust him as a Father, a Daddy. He was asking me to live as a little girl in need.

What little girl who has a good father wakes up worried, wondering if her father will come through—with food on the table, time to play, behavior that is appropriate? No trusting little girl does that. She simply wakes up, free to be the princess of the day. Or an adventuring pirate. Or a doctor healing her sick stuffed animals. Or a cowgirl. Or a captain. Or a singing superstar sensation. Whatever her imagination dreams up that day. For me, this new season of praying for my daily needs revealed the fact that I didn't trust God—not really, not for my physical needs.

At the end of the day, some of the burden of responsibility for my needs did land on me. Not only was I to pray and wait, but in the waiting I was also supposed to write.

I wasn't a writer. I was a teacher who loved to teach because I didn't have to sit still. Teachers get to move, talk, and interact. Writing is, well . . . sedentary. It's isolating. It's tiring, working to craft words in such a way that an imaginary reader will stay engaged and not get bored and walk away. Writing is something other people do, smarter people. Writers are people who know the difference between adverbs, prepositions, and pronouns; people who know where to put the commas. Writers never make sentences too long or too short and know you don't start sentences with and, but, with, or so, which I like to do.

Smart people are writers, not me. That wasn't a title anywhere posted on my make-me-look-great résumé. Yet that was what I felt God was asking me to do.

Pray.
Wait.
Write.
Repeat.

Every day for seven to eight months, that rhythm was my reality. Those first three words played throughout my day mingled with many, many tears. Some of you know these tears. You've shed similar ones as you've stared into hungry faces while holding the open door of an empty fridge or pantry. You've held a foreclosure notice or had the power or water shut off, again. You've prayed and prayed, wondering if the tear-filled prayers were heard, only to watch as provision "miraculously" came. Tears of fear transformed into tears of triumph as the electrical bill was paid anonymously, or a lost twenty-dollar bill surfaced, or a random check came in the mail. Daily bread provided on the day you needed it.

During this season, I learned that I had *no* desire to pray for my *daily* bread as Jesus modeled that we do. I wanted *nothing* to do with that kind of a prayer. As a blessed, affluent American, I enjoyed my regular paychecks and my needs being met on a *weekly* or *monthly* basis. This level of surrender, humility, and *daily* dependence was definitely *more* work than I had signed up for.

But I was obedient. I prayed. I waited. I watched. I wrote. And over time, this get-it-done-myself woman learned to pray and rely on God like a little girl. As bill after bill was paid randomly, anonymously, generously, and surprisingly, he went from being "God" to being "Father." Then one day I felt the name rise up in my heart . . . "Daddy." The process occurred as he one by one snipped the strings to the lies that had prevented me from being that little girl. The lies that were exposed? Here are a few:

- God doesn't care about me (another layer of that lie sliced off; lies often happen in layers).
- God is powerless to help me out in my life.
- At some point, God will leave me and abandon me.
- I am on my own financially, and God will be of no help to me.
- God just wants to use me, that is why he is helping me.
- I'm just his workhorse.

- I'm not worthy (or good enough) to be loved by God.
- God is like my earthly father; he will leave and abandon me.
- God is a dictator like my stepfather; he will make demands and then hurt me.
- God won't change my circumstances.
- God won't fulfill my desires.
- God won't meet my unfulfilled longings.
- God will use my past to haunt me.
- God will never use me for good.
- God won't heal my loneliness.
- God wants to punish me for my choices/decisions.
- God won't fix my problems.

Guess that was more than a few. Those are the lies that this big ask exposed, the lies that kept me from being a little girl—free to trust and free to play in Daddy's arms.

I think for a man or a woman pursuing healthy sexuality, this is a vital lesson. To feel comfortable as a woman, I had to start by learning to be comfortable as a little girl. Lies had to be replaced with truth. I had to learn that in all my girlieness, I was not too much. My emotions weren't too much. In all the ways I had felt unsafe as a little girl, I had to learn that I was safe—safe enough to try, explore, and finally emotionally grow up into more. Learning God was safe allowed me to risk again learning to be a girl.

A truth I believe to my core: if I never felt safe enough to be a girl, I would never feel safe enough to do the *more* work needed to become a healthy woman. There would always be something that had to be addressed and healed in my past before I could live free in the present and from a place of powerful purpose in the future.

This season of pray, wait, and write allowed me to become that little girl again as I waited on Daddy to pay my bills. It gave me the opportunity to renounce the lies and embrace new truths, truths that helped shape and free my Christlike identity. These truths even brought about such changes as me loving the color pink, especially bright pink. It's now my favorite color. Pale pink is nice too, but bright pink . . . that's where it's at.

Liking the color pink might sound like a trivial thing to mention. But it's evidence of the transformation that renouncing lies and embracing truth can bring. Growing up as a girl, I *hated* pink. Pink represented girly, and the lies told me it wasn't safe to be girly, that I wasn't good enough at being girly. So why even try?

I like pink now and a host of other new things. All because I've had the opportunity to take a long, hard look at things that I believed back in my early, formative years. This journey of healing childhood wounds wasn't easy. It was painful. It took work. It took programs like those mentioned and many others filled with great curriculum and healing experiences. Each, in different ways, at different times, helped peel back layers of wounds and free the lies trapped inside that I was believing about God.

So far I've addressed lies about God, about women, and even a few about myself here and there. Now to the other challenging ones—the lies about men.

Fill in the Blank

Would you humor me for a second and try something? Would you fill in the following blanks with the first word(s) that comes to your mind?

All men are _____.

Men are _____.

Men will always _____.

Men never _____.

Men only _____.

191

How'd you do? What'd you come up with? How I've filled in the blanks has affected my life greatly. For most of my life, I lived with the blanks filled in like this:

All men are <u>bad</u>.

Men are <u>selfish, narcissistic jerks</u>.

Men will always <u>hurt and abandon you</u>.

Men never <u>fight for you</u>.

Men only <u>want sex and will do whatever to whomever to get it</u>.

Pretty awful list, eh? That's what I believed because, in most cases, it's what I experienced. But do you notice something I just said? In most cases—*not all.*

I was living with a set of black-and-white judgmental accusations that condemned all men based on the actions of a few. Granted, those few men were pretty key figures in my life, which is why their actions affected me so deeply. Your reality is the only truth you know until you give yourself the opportunity to experience a new one, and those experiences were my reality. Why risk pain, abandonment, and abuse again? It's easier to hide behind the judgments and the lies. You get to stay safe and secure there, especially when the lies are buried so deep you don't even realize you are living by them.

Sadly, some of you reading this really get it. You've been sexually abused and have had parts of your soul taken from you that you don't know if you will ever get back. This brings me back to the question: Do you believe that he is able?

He has been able to bring healing and restoration to my wounds so far. The lies that enslaved me to fear all men don't imprison me like they used to. Having the opportunity to do life with the godly men in my community the past seven years has helped me see that not all men are _____. I try not to use those statements anymore. Instead, I say, some men are _____, but other men are _____, and God will protect me and help me to know the difference between the two.

There are men who are godly and good and simply try to wake up every day and do life the right way. They are men who take their role as protectors seriously and get just as enraged at predatory men as I do. They are men who pray for me, hug me, challenge me, and have fun with me. They are men who look for and call forth the best in me, the godly woman God has made me to be. They are also the men in your life who want nothing more than to be agents of protection and provision and ambassadors of God's love. They are the men worthy of the name men.

The tragedy? For decades,

- Lies kept me from being in community with men like that.
- Lies kept me in a pattern of being self-protective instead of letting good men be agents of protection.
- Lies kept me from continuing to date men as the subconscious lies would cause me to push away, turn, and run in terror and fear.
- Lies kept me trying to lead and control instead of being willing to follow.
- Lies made me prideful and caused me to do things such as carry something too heavy, even when a gentleman nearby offered to help.
- Lies caused me to want to be a man, so I wouldn't risk being hurt by one.
- Lies made me judge men for being shallow, selfish, overly sexual, and in pursuit of power, all the while being those things myself.

There's another truth I had to learn to factor in: "God created man in his own image" (Gen. 1:27).

Do you see the challenge in that? If all men are bad, then ultimately God, who created them, is bad. He made them in his image. If their image is bad, so is his. This means I've had to do the *more* work of giving men the opportunity to be good in my life. Again, it has been *more* work. It has been scary, deprogramming-of-the-heart-and-mind kind of work.

I acknowledge that reading the previous sentence just ruffled some feathers. Saying someone with a same-sex attraction is in need of deprogramming isn't quite PC these days. You or someone you know is attracted to the same sex, and there isn't any de- or reprogramming that is needed. There was no trauma, no abuse, no abandonment in your story as in mine. In the great debate over nature versus nurture, there is nothing that points to a cause of same-sex attraction. If there was never a cause, then there is no need for a solution. From birth, the attraction has been present. This may be true. And there may or may not be any trauma of woven lies, wounds, and fear that, mixed together, led you or someone you know down the same-sex road.

We all are born with a prideful, selfish, and sinful nature. No one has to teach a toddler to bite, scream "Mine!," or throw a tantrum on the floor. Those are the result of being born with a sinful heart that needs saving. Regardless of the sin nature, what caused it, or the ways we validate it, God asks for permission to save us from that heart and for us to work alongside the Holy Spirit to wage war and resist the temptation to sin, which I believe acting on same-sex desires is.

This last statement needs some clarification. It's not a sin to be tempted. The book of Hebrews tells us that Jesus was tempted in every way and that because he was, we don't have to hide our desires from him. Instead, we can step toward him in hope of help, without worry. Jesus understands. He gets the wants, the temptations, and the desires. The carrot in front of us, dangling the opportunity to sin—he gets it. Since he was able to say no, he can provide a way for us to say no, as well as comfort us in our struggle. He too faced down the temptation to sin.

> For we do not have a high priest who is unable to empathize with
> our weaknesses, but we have one who has been tempted in every

way, just as we are—yet he did not sin. Let us then approach God's throne of grace with confidence, so that we may receive mercy and find grace to help us in our time of need. (Heb. 4:15–16 NIV)

For some of you, acting on same-sex desires isn't a sin in your mind. If it is, how is it different from any other sin? Is it really that bad? Isn't there grace? Listen to Paul's answer:

You say, "I am allowed to do anything"—but not everything is good for you. And even though "I am allowed to do anything," I must not become a slave to anything. . . .

Don't you realize that your bodies are actually parts of Christ? Should a man take his body, which is part of Christ, and join it to a prostitute? Never! And don't you realize that if a man joins himself to a prostitute, he becomes one body with her? For the Scriptures say, "The two are united into one." But the person who is joined to the Lord is one spirit with him.

Run from sexual sin! No other sin so clearly affects the body as this one does. For sexual immorality is a sin against your own body. Don't you realize that your body is the temple of the Holy Spirit, who lives in you and was given to you by God? You do not belong to yourself, for God bought you with a high price. *So you must* honor God with your body. (1 Cor. 6:12, 15–20 NLT, emphasis added)

So. You. Must. A three-word combination I hate, thank you very much.

I *must* honor God with my body? I must. He gets to be the King. He gets to make the requests. I am simply asked to obey and trust my Father with the rules. Friend, whether you like guys or girls or however you are tempted to check the box, honoring God with your body is tough! It's hard! My mind and my body always want to partner together to talk me into doing things I shouldn't. Gay or straight, you know this challenge.

Let me speak a moment to those of you who have same-sex desires who want to want what God wants but who don't want to be alone the rest of your life. It is hard and can be depressing as you weigh what following God on this issue might cost. Entrusting your desires to God might mean that you live a life of celibacy. I know that some will pipe up and say that there are worse things than being celibate for life. I'm sure there are. But the thought of living a life in which those desires are never fulfilled is difficult. At least it has been for me. I had a friend ask me just yesterday why so many Christians who struggle with same-sex desires go back into the lifestyle. My answer? #thestruggleisreal.

The struggle is very real. When your mind and body are screaming yes, it is *more* work to connect to the Spirit and choose no. It's *more* work than most want to do. But with everything I've experienced while journeying on the way of hope, I have learned it is a hope worth striving for. One obedient no has provided more peace and more joy than a thousand wrong yeses ever have. King David's words are true:

> You make known to me the path of life;
>> in your presence there is fullness of joy;
>> at your right hand are pleasures forevermore. (Ps. 16:11)

In his presence alone, beholding him, there is fullness of joy. There is, *with him*, fullness of joy—nowhere else and in nothing else.

You must fight through and *not* believe the lies, then do the *more* work of believing the truth—that *his love alone* is enough. And, friend, I do believe that it is. Yes, having secondary loves around me is nice. I love feeling loved by people. But the past seven years of journeying have taught me, through many dark nights of the soul, that his love is better. I can remain single the rest of my life and be more blessed and more loved than by lying next to any human being.

For today, seeking his presence helps me feel the love and joy my soul has always hungered for. No gay or straight relationship has ever brought anything close to that.

Notice that I said *for today*. I've learned that to survive the sexual and mental battles, I must live inside today. I can do single today. It's when I stare past the twenty-four hours before me and take on the fears, insecurities, and desires of tomorrow, next year, or a decade from now that my faith starts to weaken. I don't want to be alone, so I fret, worry, wonder. I listen to fears that four days ago I would not have entertained. I start to control, to waver on my real identity. I start to doubt God.

In Matthew 6, Jesus specifically warns against this type of thinking and living. "But seek first his kingdom and his righteousness, and all these things will be given to you as well. Therefore do not worry about tomorrow, for tomorrow will worry about itself. Each day has enough trouble of its own" (vv. 33–34 NIV).

Notice how Jesus words it. He says "do not." He doesn't say "try not to" or "do your best not to." No, he says "do not."

I often blow past the "do not," thinking that it's not that big of a deal. But it is. I think it can be a life or death kind of a big deal.

When trying to break free from any pattern of sin, brokenness, anxiety, or fear, this is one of the most important verses a person can live out. For the next hour or twenty-four hours, I can trust God. I can seek him in this minute, this hour, this day. I trust him to add into my life the things that are best for me. His kingdom comes first, not mine.

It's when my pride and self-centeredness glance beyond the barriers of the next twenty-four hours and attempt to control, contrive, or manipulate my tomorrow, next week, or next year that I end up in sin, shame, despair, and depression.

I acknowledge that this is hard; it takes *more* work. It's the *more* work I am having to do even today. I try not to worry and whine and question whether I will be single the rest of my life. As I write this chapter, another birthday sits four days away. I had hoped this year would be the year that I would meet a guy able to look past my past and see the redeemed me.

Yes, I said guy, as of the male persuasion. If you remember, I was attracted to their species before. For me, as a result of deep emotional and spiritual healing work, heterosexual attraction has returned. Restoration of this hot-mess creation has occurred, which is what I believe God longs to do for all of us—restore us to his original design.

Jesus points to the concept of original design as he talks to the Pharisees. He addresses the controversial issue of divorce by having the Pharisees look back at God's original design and saying in so many words, "Go back to that." Go back to fulfilling God's original design, not yours. Go back to two becoming one. Go back to commitment. That's what I want you to do.

> And Pharisees came up to him and tested him by asking, "Is it lawful to divorce one's wife for any cause?" He answered, "Have you not read that he who created them from the beginning made them male and female, and said, 'Therefore a man shall leave his father and his mother and hold fast to his wife, and the two shall become one flesh'? So they are no longer two but one flesh. What therefore God has joined together, let not man separate." (Matt. 19:3–6)

From the Beginning . . .

I believe that these are the three most important words Jesus spoke on the topic of sex and sexuality, because they take us back to the beginning, back to Genesis and to the Garden of Eden, the garden where Adam was *whom God created*. God gave Adam the job of naming all the animals *God created*. God noticed that none of them were fit to help Adam, and because it wasn't good for Adam to be alone, God, *the Creator*, created woman, Eve, for Adam. Eve for Adam and Adam for Eve, and the two became one.

This is the original created design, designed by the original Creator. God invites heterosexuals to step back from divorcing and move toward the original created design. I believe he invites those in same-sex relationships to move toward the original created design as well.

The Creator invites us *all* back to the created order. John Ortberg reminds us in *The Me I Want to Be* that when something goes wrong with creation, God has not only a desire but also a way to make things right: "God doesn't make anything and then decide to throw it away. He creates, and then, if there is a problem, he rescues. Redemption always involves the redemption of creation."[5]

Throughout my healing journey, that's what I've experienced—rescue, restoration, and redemption. So, yes, I am again attracted to men. With that attraction comes the *more* work of pushing through fears, renouncing tempting lies, and entrusting God with my heart, today. Will same-sex desires surface again one day? I don't know, which is an answer I can live with. Today has enough worries of its own. I've learned that it doesn't serve me to wonder about my sexuality or my relational status of tomorrow.

But it's tempting. As my birthday peeks its head around the corner, I am tempted to despair and get depressed. I am tempted to want things I shouldn't or take matters into my own hands. I am tempted to listen again to the voice that wants me to think I will never make it. I will never be the girl good enough, pretty enough, or healed enough to get the guy. The lies and fears can get so loud. Once again, #thestruggleisreal. And that's okay. I am a fool if I think my life here will ever see a day when it's easy. Scripture makes it clear that for those who are truly Christ-followers, the journey will be difficult, even when walking the way of hope. But there is hope.

You can hope. Despite your struggle, your sin, your shame, your guilt, or your pain, you too can hope.

Despite where you are on your faith journey, you are only one renounced lie away from experiencing more joy than you've previously known. The question remains: Will you do the *more* work that transformation requires? Will you be brave and step forward into the new you the world has never known before?

10

The Way of Bravery

We have to be braver than we think we can be, because God is constantly calling us to be more than we are.

Madeleine L'Engle[1]

There are so many ways to be brave in this world. Sometimes bravery involves laying down your life for something bigger than yourself, or for someone else. Sometimes it involves giving up everything you have ever known, or everyone you have ever loved, for the sake of something greater.

But sometimes it doesn't.

Sometimes it is nothing more than gritting your teeth through pain, and the work of every day, the slow walk toward a better life.

That is the sort of bravery I must have now.

Veronica Roth[2]

The bravest thing I ever did was continuing my life when I wanted to die.

Juliette Lewis[3]

I'm sitting outside as the December chill nips at my fingertips and my nose. I have on two pairs of pants, a long-sleeve shirt, two fleece jackets, and a wool beanie. I refuse to head inside until my fingers are so numb I can't type, which I fear will happen too soon.

Some of you reading this might not understand. Your December weather always involves freezing temperatures and snow, and sitting outside without the aid of a hot tub or fire pit is impossible. You're the inside type who doesn't need more than a walk to the mailbox to get your fill of sunshine. Me, well, I think you already know me well enough to know what I like, if you've been reading and paying attention, that is.

I find myself rambling as I struggle with how to move on. How do I put into words how different your life can be when what you believed crumbles as truth takes hold?

Now, seven years later, I am not who I used to be. The monster that frightened me I now understand and have compassion for. The wounded little girl I no longer hide and blame. The lives I used to live are not me anymore. I'm not the judgmental Christian enslaved to legalism and perfection. I'm not the addicted, same-sex-desiring codependent. I'm not the workaholic, approval addict either.

I'm me.

I'm a woman in progress whose journey has been harder and more graphic than paper and ink can hold. Life is better now. There's more joy. Most of all, there's more peace. I have peace. The thing most people would kill for I know I have—peace.

Yes, my feathers still get ruffled over this and that from time to time, but it's not the anxiety-driven, not-knowing-who-I-am, lost-identity kind of lack of peace. I've beheld him beholding me, and seeing that much love solidified a heart-level foundation of peace.

As I look back on my journey, I see that what changed my behavior the most was changing what I believed. What changed my beliefs was changing what I beheld. One led to another and then another. As I have journeyed on the way of hope, the beat of the rhythm has changed me: beholding, believing, behaving.

Nothing else. I wonder if that wasn't the same rhythm that Jesus walked to—beholding his Father, becoming secure in his beliefs, behaving in perfection.

Looking around, I realize how fortunate I am. I have had opportunities and experiences that seem rare. I don't think they are supposed to be. Maybe this is the kind of healing work God wants to do in everyone, if we would only be more willing and believe that he is able and be braver. To change how I behaved required me to be brave enough to change what I believed. As my beliefs changed, I had to be brave enough to let my behavior change as well.

Let me explain. People around you expect you to show up as you were the day before or when they last saw you. But Jesus can change you. Radically. It may happen in an instant or more slowly, one degree at a time. Either way, it's change. And change makes people uncomfortable. Most people don't want you to change. They like you to stay as you are. They have you boxed and labeled in a way that makes them comfortable. They label you so they can relate to you or not, all depending on the label.

I hate labels. I still get asked if I am gay or straight. People want to label you so they can check off a box. I've learned that only one box matters.

☑ Daughter of the King

That's my box. If I check that box and let that label drive my identity, then I am okay. But that takes bravery. It takes bravery to believe it. It takes bravery to feel it. It takes bravery to live it. It takes bravery to live a life of freedom and power. That kind of change and bravery makes people nervous. It challenges their lives of sameness and mediocrity. That's not for me. I don't believe that's for you either.

Today, you are being invited to be brave: brave in beholding God in a new way, brave in taking hold of new beliefs, and brave as you let your new beliefs drive new behaviors.

- When you start to feel softer, you are brave and dress softer.
- When you feel prettier, you are brave and start to dress prettier.
- When you feel more protected, you are brave and step outside your box and do something adventurous.
- When you believe you're worthy, you are brave and lift your head up and make eye contact with someone walking by.
- When you stop hating the opposite sex, you are brave enough to become friends.
- When you start becoming attracted to the opposite sex again, you are brave enough to talk to a person you are attracted to and not hide from them the entire night, or month, or year.
- When you stop believing you have to be perfect, you stop acting perfectly, or dressing the kids perfectly, or killing yourself to do your job perfectly.
- If you continue to be attracted to someone of the same sex, you are brave enough to own it and work through the needed boundaries to protect both of you.
- When you start to see that people with same-sex attractions have a heart and a story, you are brave enough to reach out and befriend them.
- When you start to see that not all people in the church are bad, you are brave enough to reach out and befriend a Christian or attend a church.

As I continue my journey down the way of hope, the one thing I've discovered is that daily I have to get my brave on. I have to be brave in owning my story. I have to be brave in owning my struggles. I have to be brave in stepping out and working through my dating fears. I have to be brave and not judge people before they might judge me. I have to be brave and let people love me. Today, I have to be brave and continue writing. These are just a few of my daily brave needs.

Most of all, I have to be brave in asking for help. Without a doubt, I need the church to continue being the church around me. I need community just as much now as I ever have before. This woman is still prone to wander, to listen to and entertain lies; therefore, I need my community speaking truth to me. I still want to default to self-protection and pride. I still want to write, or work, or hustle for the praise of people or let a secondary love be my primary. Those are temptations that still lie in me. I need to be brave enough to keep people close to me who will challenge me when I waver.

And when (not if, but *when*) my behavior starts to waver, I have to be brave enough to start the process all over again and ask myself the following: What version of God is the deep-down part of me beholding and seeing? What version of myself am I seeing? Is it an old picture with a crusty eight-track tape playing in the background of my life's worst hits? What is my still-being-sanctified heart being tempted to believe? I must be brave enough to confess those false versions of God, myself, men, or women and the lies that I am tempted to believe. Friends, regardless of how long you've been on your faith journey, confession requires bravery.

I must be brave enough to be uncomfortable, as Brené Brown reminds us: "You can choose courage or you can choose comfort. You cannot choose both."[4] On this journey, in this land that is not my home, I must remember that I can't be comfortable and grow. As much as I hate it, I must be brave enough to step into the liminal space to which God so often beckons us, that place of deep waters, away from the shore, where his hand is the only one we will have to hold. I must be brave enough to swim out to him.

Most of all, I need to be brave enough to hope. In this life, there is nothing more powerful than hope, but it takes someone brave to hope. It takes someone brave to let hope take such root that they begin to believe. It takes someone brave to believe so strongly that they are able to wait.

Or work
Or speak
Or write
Or date
Or dance
Or dream

It takes a brave person to let hope renew the ability to dream. It takes bravery to dream of a second chance. It takes bravery to dream of a renewed life. It takes bravery to dream of the fulfillment of an old dream.

Our God of hope is the God of second chances. He's the God of second stories. Me, I'm embarking on mine.

Now it's your turn. Grab your cape of courage and embark on your second story. Journey bravely down the way of hope.

Epilogue

Views from the Other Side of the Fence

A Mother's Perspective

As you just read from my story, I've been all over the map when it comes to God, church, same-sex attraction, and same-sex marriage. Because of my experiences, people who are friends or family members of those in the LGBT lifestyle or struggling with same-sex attraction often reach out to me, seeking help, advice, and so forth on how to best love and walk alongside their loved one. I always wish I had more wisdom to offer, as I don't actually know what it is like to be on the other side of the fence, trying to love someone whose sexual preferences, identity, or choices aren't what you and/or they would want for them.

What I do know is that it isn't easy. I know at different points in my journey I was *very* difficult—even impossible—to love, as I pushed people away out of anger, pain, shame, fear, and every other reason or emotion you could consider. I didn't want people around me if I felt they had hurt me, or would hurt or reject me, because of the choices I was making. Yes, I enjoyed playing the victim in my story, blaming others for the pain they had or could cause me.

Especially my mother.

I spent many, many years pushing her out of my life. First, emotionally when I started living a life I knew she wouldn't approve of, then physically when I thought her actions had so wronged me she didn't deserve grace or forgiveness or to be a part of my life.

She may not have all the right answers, and you may not always agree with her, but I want you to hear from her directly about the difficulties she faced trying to love someone as challenging to love as me.

Our relationship has definitely been a roller coaster, with its share of ups and downs, and at times it still is. Thankfully, she has never given up trying to love me. Most of all, I know she never gave up praying for me.

I hope by hearing tales from her side of the fence you too can find cause to hope in a God who is not done yet. After all, whomever it is that you love, God loves them too.

ME: *Because my journey took place at a time when same-sex relationships were not culturally acceptable, I tried to hide my sexuality struggles and choices from you. Which makes me wonder, when did you know?*

Mother: I suspected during college. When you brought friends home, there were moments when I saw strange behaviors that made me wonder. Every time you brought a new friend home I would wonder. I couldn't prove anything and didn't want to. I didn't have the courage to ask. Deep down I knew what was going on, but I didn't want to admit it to myself or have to confront it, much less have to decide what to do about it. The wondering and agonizing over your actions and what might be going on was hard to process. You see, when you were a little girl, you always wanted me to read the Bible to you. That was so unusual that I felt you were an angel God had chosen to do great things for him. I couldn't figure out how someone so seemingly pure and close to God could or would choose something outside of what I believed God had for you. I realize you weren't pure (none of us are), but your "talk" was so filled with "perfection" back then that it seemed at times that you were. Little did I know, you were crumbling inside.

ME: Knowing the effect perfectionism had on me, I wonder, Mom, what was it like for you being raised in a home where you were expected to be perfect? How did that affect you as you tried to parent me?

Mother: I was raised by a very loving, God-fearing mother. She was definitely a perfectionist, and children were expected to be perfect. My mother was wonderful, and I thought she was perfect. I know she did her very best. As I became a young mother, I listened to every piece of advice and tried to make you and your sister perfect too. It took me a few years to figure out there are no perfect children (or people for that matter). When I was growing up, the bar was high, especially as an only child, which I was. Every drink had to have a coaster under it, things couldn't be left out of place, and every pan had to be scoured with an SOS pad after cooking. That was just in the home. When out in public, at church or wherever, it felt as if every i had to be dotted and every t crossed. We had to be perfect. I have often wondered where she learned this. I've also wondered why being in control, about *everything*, was such an overpowering need and force in her life. As Mother aged, I filled in a few blanks about her life that made some things clearer. Her sibling before and after her died, and it had a profound impact on her. Perhaps she felt if she didn't keep everything under control, something else bad would happen. However, I didn't realize how this affected me until my late thirties when everything fell apart. Our family was in great disarray. When Mother and Daddy would come to visit, I would be a basket case because I was so afraid she would see through the perfect family act I was putting on.

I remember distinctly the weekend they came to the house and then left before church on Sunday because we didn't go to the "right" church. When I got out of church, I started sobbing uncontrollably. All the pressure of trying to make it look right had finally taken its toll. The adrenaline that my life and my heart had been running on had finally run out. It's then that I started counseling, and I thought a couple of visits would prove to be the "quick fix" that I needed in my life. After several sessions with my counselor, he helped me see that despite decades of sitting in church, I didn't actually have a personal relationship with God. I was just trying to please my parents. I hadn't realized it before, but subconsciously, I felt that if I pleased my mother and father, then God was bound to be happy with me. That's when I started on my journey to find my own faith. My journey through my own personal wilderness, which as you know included horrific mistakes and dark moments of hell, was the hardest thing I've ever been through. It included watching you walk down a dark path and being alienated from you. But now I am thankful for the journey, because it was in this wilderness that the chains of perfectionism were broken, and I truly found God there.

ME: *In this home of perfectionism, did you ever struggle with feeling loved by your mother? Was she nurturing? Physically affectionate? Was she a hugger? Was your father? I believe that many people who have same-sex attractions have a high need for physical affection. I don't think I got enough. What was it like for you growing up?*

Mother: I don't remember being hugged a lot by my mother and never by my father. Despite the lack of physical affection, I did know that they both loved me. In that day and age, men weren't affectionate, at least from what I saw and experienced. It wasn't until I was grown and married that I realized I probably really needed that from Daddy. I don't hold it against him as I know he would have done anything for me.

As for you and your sister, I couldn't have loved you more. I am sure I didn't show it perfectly, but you both were my world. I don't know how it was perceived by you though. It may be that after the divorce, you girls were so hurt that you shut down and couldn't feel my love. I remember thinking during the divorce that I loved you so much and that my love was enough and that you would get through it just fine. It also may be that my deep depression after the divorce kept me from being able to show my love. I am sorry that you may not have had enough affection, but I hope you know the love was there even if the dark clouds might have overshadowed it.

ME: In my journey, I've countless times asked myself, "Why?" Why am I struggling with this? What's one question that you wrestled with as you watched me struggle with this attraction?

Mother: "What did I do wrong?"

I felt I had done so many things wrong, and there was no way to fix any of them. When I was in the midst of the divorce and remarriage, my mother told me I was going to hell for the choices I was making, and I might be taking others with me. During that time, I worried over what I had done wrong and feared Mother's words were coming true and that my sins were being visited on you.

The next logical question was, "What can I do to fix it?" The only answer I came up with was to pray. But that didn't seem like enough.

ME: What would you say to a family member or friend who feels that same way? That their prayers aren't enough.

Mother: Prayer is probably the only thing that works. God loves your family member more than you do, and sometimes getting out of the way is the best thing to do. If we try to get in the way of God working in their heart, that can be detrimental. It is very hard to wait on God, because we can't control their choices or whether they choose to walk down the safer path God has for them. Waiting is what we are told to do as Psalm 5:3 reminds us: "In the morning, LORD, you hear my voice; in the morning I lay my requests before you and wait expectantly" [NIV].

ME: What would you say to a family member or friend who is struggling to wait on God? I can only imagine how hard it was to wait on God during the dark periods when I wouldn't talk to you or couldn't have cared less about God.

Mother: Eat a lot of chocolate.

No, seriously, there aren't words to describe how painful that was during the years you wouldn't talk to me. It was like grieving the death of a child, and my purpose for living was over. I couldn't even clean the house. There were too many memories of you that stabbed me in the heart. It was like part of me died.

I learned a lot about waiting and wandering in the wilderness from my Christian counselor and that at times the best thing I could do was to just put one foot in front of the other. One day in our ladies Bible class, we were studying worry, and the leader of the class had an exercise for us to do that changed everything.

We were given a sheet of paper and told to write the top three things we were worried about. You were at the top of the list. We were then told to write the *result* of that worry. It hit me like a bolt of lightning that all my agony and worry had not changed a thing. I let it go and let God have it that day. In that moment, I surrendered it and started waiting on God. It truly was a moment of divine intervention. God, in that moment, really did take away all that anxiety I was exhausted from carrying, and for the first time in years I had a moment of peace.

Bottom line, as parents, family members, friends, we aren't in control. Worrying won't change anything. The only thing it will change is the number of wrinkles on your skin. Praying really does change things. And yes, it *always* takes longer than we want to wait. But still we must wait. We must trust. We must give God a chance to be God and stop trying to be God ourselves.

While we wait, we need to love. Continue to love the person, love ourselves by taking care of ourselves, and love others by sharing the light of Christ. Putting God first and spending time in his presence will enable us to wait in love.

ME: *You mentioned loving the person. How do you do that? As a family member or friend, how do you love the person well without condoning or condemning?*

Mother: [Sigh] Since I took the road of pretending it wasn't true, I didn't have to openly say anything. There was an instance years ago when you and Kristi were in the car, and you were playing a comedy CD by Ellen. I chastised you for buying something of hers because of her lifestyle. I was talking about how radical the LGBT agenda was becoming, and I instantly saw your displeasure at my comments. I knew I had made my point, but I also knew I needed to stop or it would damage our relationship. In hindsight, I would not have made those comments. From where I stand now, I would have sat down with you and discussed openly the situation and expressed my feelings and concerns that you were not walking down the path God had for you. I would also have expressed that you were my child and that I loved you unconditionally, even though I didn't believe what you were doing was what God wanted for you.

I do acknowledge that I had it easier in some ways because you weren't open and physically affectionate in front of me. I don't know how I would have handled that. It's hard to love people where they are when "where they are" is something you don't understand or presses strongly on something that you believe not to be the best for them. If you had been that open, I think I would have expressed my love but also expressed a need for boundaries: "I am not comfortable with physical affection in front of me and ask that you not do it."

ME: *What would you say to a family member or friend whose loved one wants to bring their boyfriend/girlfriend or partner into the home or to family functions?*

Mother: As a Christ-follower, I believe we are to love the sinner, not the sin. I would make them feel welcome in my home but also lovingly explain that I don't condone their choice or lifestyle. I acknowledge that in theory this sounds simple but in real life is a very painful and hard process to live out. It requires much prayer and trusting God to give you the words for the difficult conversations and grace when words slip out that are a mistake.

I know several people who have faced this, and they went on loving their children as well as welcoming their partners into their homes. I am confident they showed great love to all involved while not sacrificing their beliefs. It isn't easy, but we were never promised an easy road, only that he would be with us while we walked down it.

ME: *What would you say to a parent feeling guilt or shame for any mistakes they've made along the way?*

Mother: If there is anything you know you did wrong, then take the steps to apologize and right the wrong if possible. You must then move forward and put it in the past. Satan will tell you that you are not worthy. For years, I felt so guilty over my choices that I shouldn't darken the doors of a church. However, I went and took you and your sister because I did not want you to go to hell. Eventually, I found a very loving, grace-filled, godly church community who helped love me back to spiritual health. It took years, but I thank God for them. I realized along the way that I couldn't change the past, but I could try to live for God and share his love with others.

ME: *Was there any certain Scripture verse or passage that helped you get through either your depression or the season when I was* *estranged from you, or that helped you break free from guilt and shame that might help someone move forward in their own journey of faith?*

Mother: The Psalms were my go-to place. During my depression, when it was really bad, I couldn't read, pray, listen, or anything. As I improved, I spent a lot of time in the Psalms. What has helped me live free from the guilt is from 2 Corinthians 12:9:

> But he said to me, "My grace is sufficient for you, for my power is made perfect in weakness." Therefore I will boast all the more gladly about my weaknesses, so that Christ's power may rest on me.

Hearing Paul's words, "My grace is sufficient," and realizing that grace really is able to cover all my mistakes has given me freedom to carry on guilt-free.

But my favorite verses are Isaiah 48:17–18:

> This is what the LORD says—
>   your Redeemer, the Holy One of Israel:
> "I am the LORD your God,
>   who teaches you what is best for you,
>   who directs you in the way you should go.
> If only you had paid attention to my commands,
>   your peace would have been like a river,
>   your well-being like the waves of the sea." [NIV]

One day when I was in the middle of the mess of my life, I stumbled upon that passage, and it was an aha moment for me. It was as if God said, "If you would have just listened, you wouldn't be in this mess. You would have peace."

That made me realize that all of God's commands are for our good, not just rules to follow. I realized for the first time that God's laws are for our protection from emotional and spiritual pain and danger. God had been trying to protect me all my life, but I had disregarded the little voice in me that said, "This is not what you are supposed to do" or "This will take you into big trouble."

There I was, sitting with my life (as well as yours and your sister's) in a mess. I began earnestly trying to follow his leading and to listen to his quiet voice saying, "This is the way that is right." This allows him the opportunity to protect me as I finish this life. There will be problems, as we all know, but at least they will not be self-inflicted if I follow the Lord. It has become my desire to help other people see this clearly, so they will stop and turn to the Lord and not make the mistakes I did.

But it's bigger than that. Following his path, his way, the way of hope, really will bring the peace and the joy that you are looking for.

ME: *Anything else you would like to say or want people to know?*

Mother: I want to be an EH.

ME: *Huh?*

Mother: A friend told me that at her husband's funeral, one of his coworkers who spoke at the service said that EH was the nickname they gave to her husband. She had never heard this, so she listened intently. The coworker said it stood for Enemy Hugger. She said that her husband was a very forgiving person—as soon as something happened, he forgave. At work, if someone did something wrong, he would talk with them and then hug them. I am convinced there is not near enough forgiveness in the world.

I was thinking about a couple I knew who were having trouble, and the Lord placed this on my heart: "Resentment ruins relationships, so forgive." That is my other message to the world. I know how blessed I was to be forgiven, and I can do no less for others. Go hug your enemy and make peace!

May his grace and peace be with you!

The Daddy/Daughter Dance

As I write this section, two slices into my self-indulgent, medicating pepperoni pizza, I realize that my heart hurts. I find myself wishing I had stayed home to write so the snotty tears that want to fall would have a safer place to land than in public. I also find myself wanting to order another beer to numb the pain that I feel.

The pain comes as I reflect on the Daddy/daughter dance. Many daughters have memories of dances or dates with their fathers tucked away in the scrapbook of their lives. A daughter standing on her father's toes as they sway in sync back and forth. Dances in the living room to practice and prepare for the prom. Photos of a father of the bride and daughter in white dancing as the teary-eyed mother of the bride stands aside.

Moments. Memories. Story lines that should fill every page of a princess daughter's storybook life. In my story, the dance between my father and me has been anything but picturesque.

There are more empty pages in the scrapbook than filled ones. At times, the only dance steps taken were ones in which we stepped on each other's toes by the choices of our lives.

This might be the section of the book I am most proud of, because when it comes to my father and me, we are still working and trying to get this dance of a relationship right. Neither of us has quit, despite the many reasons the other has provided. Which is nice, because I am not the girl I used to be. He definitely isn't the man he was before, and this book has provided a beautiful dance floor for us to come together again and see what happens next.

Yes, God has opened the door this year for us to sit down and really hear the other, which has never happened before. We both carried too many wounds that would spill out, mess up the dance floor, and cause the other to trip.

Thankfully, God kept the music playing, and we now have the opportunity for a new song, a redo, and the hope for more: more from God, more from ourselves, more from the other. God is working to restore the more that we both long for. But it's not easy. At times, I've wanted to take off my dance shoes and walk away. At times, I have. Yet God finds a way to turn us back around and encourages us to try again on the dance floor of our lives. For those of you who may think healing and restoration inside a relationship are beyond God's reach, keep praying and listening. He can bring the unlikeliest of people back together, people like Pops (as I like to call my dad now) and me.

I asked Pops to share a little bit about his story and what he's learned on his journey of trying to love God and love me more.

ME: *What was it like for you growing up?*

Pops: I grew up in what I believe to be one of the best eras someone could grow up in, 1946 to 1964. Life was simpler. Richer. I lived with my mother and father and three sisters, and things at home were good. My dad worked hard in retail, and from a very young age, we kids would get done with school and chores and then head to the store to help Dad with restocking, cleaning, or whatever needed to be done. This "work hard and help the family" mentality wasn't to be questioned and was just what we did at that time. I see how it taught me to work hard and provide for my own needs. The only area I really saw my mom and dad disagree on was church, as they would often argue on what denomination my sisters and I would go to. This instilled in me at a very young age that when I got married, attending one church together would be very, very important.

ME: If you could go back in time, what would you do differently?

Pops: First, I would say that, in hindsight, I did not realize how my work affected everyone. Yes, I was a dedicated and hard worker, which I learned at a very young age. But as I look back, I see that I should have worked smarter. If you go back as far as middle school, I was in the workforce for fifty-five years, and throughout those years, I put my work first. My priorities were wrong. Family should have come first, in both my first and second marriage. Somewhere during my first marriage, I began to believe that I wasn't good enough or not a good provider, so I threw myself into work to prove that lie wrong.

I also had the opportunity to stay in Texas and work rather than moving to Colorado when you were in high school and your sister was in college. Again, I put my work and my role as a provider first. I often wonder how things might have turned out differently had I stayed in Texas.

ME: What was it like being a father and not having a close relationship with your daughter?

Pops: Not getting to have a relationship with you was by far the hardest thing I have had to bear in my life. During the divorce, I fought for custody of you and your sister. Right before the divorce was final, through many prayers, I came to realize that girls belong with their mom. I didn't want to take you away from her and the needs you had that only she could meet. Believe me, there were many prayers about this decision. I ended up with joint custody, but things didn't go as I had planned. The joint custody wasn't as mutual or equal in time as I thought it would be, which is my fault. I should have fought harder and spoke up more. Unfortunately, I was so broken after the affair and the divorce that I didn't fight for you and your sister like you needed me to. There are so many things that have happened in your lives that I don't know if I will ever be able to forgive myself for. Throughout the years, I sought counsel from pastors of all the churches I attended. I would share how hard it was being estranged from you, and each one would tell me, "She will think things through, and when she is ready, she will reach out and healing will begin." I am so thankful for these past few months and the reconciliation that has occurred, but I am still so grieved by all the time we lost.

ME: *As we've talked about the struggles and challenges I have been through, what thoughts or perspectives do you have on it all?*

Pops: I believe your challenges, struggles, and sadness began the night I saw you in the ledge above the backseat, staring out the back window of that Chevy Impala, as your mother drove off with you and your sister to head back to central Texas. I could hear you crying and yelling, "Daddy, Daddy, Daddy," and my heart just broke. I ran after the car when I heard you screaming, but it only drove faster and sped away. I think that set off a chain of events in your life that you are still recovering from. Despite all the hard work you've done growing and healing in the Lord, I know that so much of what you've gone through was because I wasn't there for you. I wasn't there to protect and guide you as my parents did me. I have prayed and will continue to pray that God will forgive me for not being there when I was needed. After the past few months, I feel as though I have been given a second chance at life, because I've been given a second chance with you. I only hope I can move forward without disappointing you or hurting you again.

ME: *How has having a relationship with God impacted your life up until now?*

Pops: I have a great relationship with God now. During difficult seasons, I read about Job's trials and tribulations and learned from his story how to handle things and how to be strong and persevere. Matthew 17:20 and Luke 9:23–24 have also helped strengthen me. To live and follow Jesus daily on his terms is tough. Thankfully, I attend a great church that I love!

ME: *What would you say to a young father struggling to balance work, family, and marriage?*

Pops: Definitely put family and church first, then your job and work! By putting family and church first, your marriage will succeed. Do not miss a school event with your child or children. Work for companies that have the same values as you and your wife do. Put your faith in God to find a way to provide the necessary means to survive and make ends meet.

ME: *What would you say to a parent who is separated from their child or feels as if their relationship with their child is hopeless?*

Pops: Don't *ever* give up! If you think you are trying, then try harder. Fight for your children and what is best for their future and their well-being. Keep giving God a chance!

Reflections from Kristi

As you read in chapter 4, I was in a same-sex marriage with Kristi that had its very real highs and ended when I reached the lowest of my lows in life. The journey that God has taken Kristi and me on since that time, individually as well as together, is probably the one story line that I am most thankful for. God has used her to give me a glimpse of just how powerful grace and forgiveness can be, as well as to show me that prayer really does change things. God walked alongside both of us individually toward healing, and because of his healing hand, we now have a redeemed friendship. Since we both are asked questions about the redemptive work that has been done, I invited Kristi to share some thoughts so that you could hear from her directly.

ME: *For those who don't know you, can you share a brief look into your journey?*

Kristi: I was raised in the all-American family—mom, dad, two kids, and a dog! I was in church every Sunday, and my faith was deeply rooted. Though I could always seem to get into trouble, I knew right from wrong, the values my parents instilled in me, and always heard "the little voice within" even when I didn't really want to. I just liked to get attention—a lot!

But inside, I always felt different, and I didn't know what it was. During a crazy game of Truth or Dare in high school, I figured it out—I liked girls. I was dazed and confused to say the least. Being raised to believe that the desires I had were wrong, I struggled to reconcile these two aspects of my life—my faith and my feelings.

I went into hiding. I tried to hide the *real* me from my friends, my family, and even myself at times. Trying to balance the two most important, yet conflicting, desires of my heart was a constant tug-of-war. I was losing endurance; I was dying inside.

Then I met you. For many reasons, I knew I had to make a choice. I couldn't pursue my same-sex desires publicly with the conviction that I felt in my heart. But I didn't want to lose you. Who would?

The decision? I stopped listening—to God.

ME: *So what happened?*

Kristi: We embarked on a new adventure together. I fully committed my heart to our relationship. We faced life together and laughed a lot along the way. We got married, moved, built a house, and had the two most perfect dogs and two most precious cats in the world. It was great—until it wasn't.

Our split was hard on both of us. For me, it was, without a doubt, the darkest time of my life. I was hurt, I was angry, and I was completely alone. I had lost the person I wanted to spend the rest of my life with and my best friend at the same time. I tried to numb the pain with anything I could get my hands on. I never knew silence could be so deafening, darkness could be so cold. I needed help, and I needed it badly.

ME: *Where did you turn for help?*

Kristi: First, it was at this time that I finally had an open and honest conversation with my parents. Though I always knew they did not condone my choices, they were always there for me. They will never know how much being there during that time meant to me. I know it was hard for them to see me so lost.

My wounds were deep, and my anger was intense. And I was angry with God. I was angry at God because what felt natural to me was wrong. I remember screaming at him, "I don't know why I am even going to pray to you because the thing that will make my heart stop hurting you won't let me have!" But as angry as I was, I knew I was hurting and was broken. I also knew that the path of healing pointed straight to him.

That night I opened my nightstand drawer and saw something out of the corner of my eye. It was my Bible. Opening it to the book of Genesis was my first step toward healing. I had tried to read the Bible through many times in my life and had been unsuccessful. This time as I read it, I felt comforted. I understood it like I never had before. Reading the Bible became my safe space. My happy place. It was just me and God.

Since that first night of stepping back into Scripture, I read the Bible three times cover to cover. I was gaining strength, until I felt as if God was nudging me to try church again. Going back to church was not about me finding faith. My relationship with him had been renewed and had become the most important relationship in my life. Going back to church was about me learning to trust people again, which I didn't want to do. But I went and sat in the back with him.

ME: So the biggest issue you were facing was the challenge to learn to trust people again. What happened from there?

Kristi: Learning to trust people was an incredibly slow process because, if I am honest, I simply didn't trust people, period. God had to nudge me and keep nudging me until finally I saw a class being offered at Gateway that I felt I was supposed to attend. [Kristi and I attend the same church but at different campuses.]

Thankfully, I was surrounded by people there who understood me, which made it a very safe place for me at the time. It gave me a little bit of community and helped me grow in my identity in him. Life wasn't about my sexuality anymore. Life was more about him.

One powerful exercise we did in the class was on the labels we use to identify ourselves. We wrote down all the labels we were carrying about ourselves on pieces of tape and then stuck them all over our bodies. I had a ton taped on me, because there were so many lies that I believed. One lie was on my front right shoulder and read "Undesirable." On the left shoulder was "Not good enough." Another read "I am unlovable." Another, "Hurt." Another, "Broken." After we finished labeling ourselves, we were given the opportunity to remove them and place them on an old wooden cross, to exchange the lie for a label of truth. I walked up to the cross and pulled off every label except one.

The label in the middle of my chest read "Gay." I wasn't ready to pull that one off and place it on the cross. I didn't want to do it just because everyone else was. I wanted to do it when I was ready.

I went home that night and started praying about it. Up until that moment, that label had been the core of my identity. "Gay" was the way I felt, and I never thought I could experience life without it. Every day that week, when I got home from work, I went out to the backyard and talked to God. I asked him, "Why can't they just understand 'gay' is who I am? I am a good person. Why can't people just love me for who I am?"

As clear as a bell I heard him say, "I do." I started hearing a question from him: "Why can't you just trust me with this?" I would turn and ask him another question about them—other people, their views and judgments—and he would ask again, "Why can't you just trust me with this?"

Sometime that week my thinking shifted. I knew I had to give God everything. I knew I had to give him my sexuality. I don't know if I thought my sexuality had changed, but I could no longer put that label above him. I had to be *his* first. I had to put him above everything else—including my sexuality.

I said okay. I was scared to death, but I was also a little bit excited. The next week I went to class an hour early and drove around the parking lot. The minute the church door was opened I got out of my car, ran in, and ripped the "Gay" label off me and placed it on the cross. I couldn't do it fast enough. Then I fell on the floor crying.

This brings up an important point I'd love for you to hear from my heart to yours. I don't want anyone to give up a label or try to change for any other reason than that they are ready. It's okay to talk to God about it. When your heart is truly ready and willing to give up the label, that's when you experience who he really is, and that's when freedom comes.

The day that I was willing to give up that label was when my heart truly opened. I could physically feel it opening. I didn't know in that moment what the next day would look like, or the next month, or my next relationship. All I knew was that I had found someone who truly loved me. And I felt it. That became the most important thing in my life. I just wanted to be with him. Everything else in my life has been that process of removing labels and replacing them with his.

Now the label reads "Loved."

ME: I know how that one label change has transformed not only your life but also impacted our ability to have a healthy, redeemed friendship. Can you share more about what that has looked like from your side of the fence?

Kristi: Finding freedom from the labels and chains that had kept us in an unhealthy relationship gave us a chance to pursue a healthy one. Yes, it took time. Healing always does. It also took intentionality and honest communication. At times, we both had to take steps back from each other to battle the habitual codependent tendencies. We needed our own space to heal. Thankfully, God provided that space.

In the ways I was holding on too tightly to you, I was able to let go of them and know that he would take care of you. In the ways I was thirsting and trying to get you to love me, I began to realize that not only could you not love me in that capacity but also that only he could. He released us from the entanglement and the codependency that we had known.

I trusted God with the redemption of our friendship. I wasn't focusing on you. You weren't focusing on me. We were both focusing on God. He was healing our hurts, covering us in grace and mercy. His love gave us the strength to forgive each other. We were learning how to show up in our true identities with each other, which allowed us to start to truly love each other in a pure way. God truly brought beauty out of the ashes of my life, of your life, and of our friendship.

Acknowledgments

For those of you who know me well, you know this book has been a team effort that I could not have accomplished on my own. Thank you . . .

To Kirby Holmes—for saying whatever you did that day that got this book going. Your words started this mess.

To Joshua and Melissa Curtis—for enduring my hatred of cameras and photo shoots and for sharing in the field that day that sweet Esther was on her way.

To Holly Hilderbrand—for your willingness to always find a place for me to write, which started with Post-it notes on Momma T's back-porch table. Most of all, for not letting me quit.

To Meg Diehl—for helping me to understand the publishing industry and for speaking the two most important words in this project: "Just write."

To Kristi Hart—for loving details, research, project management, and Jesus. Most of all, for believing in this book enough to do all the behind-the-scenes stuff I still don't realize you do. Thank you for always believing there was good in me.

To John Burke—for working through your fears and faithfully leading Gateway Church to become a place where I could find healing and experience grace and for the ways you believed in this book and the message of hope it could bring.

To Karin Harper—for weathering the ups and downs of the last seven years with me. Without your faith and friendship, I wouldn't have been able to live the grace, truth, and hope in this book.

To my Gateway Church family and prayer team—for loving me when I didn't know I was loveable and for giving me a place to grow in faith and spread my wings.

To Mom and Pops—for believing in this book enough to let the secrets out of the vault and, most of all, for loving me still.

And Kristi—remind me to schedule more events where someone gives me a really big fish.

Lastly, to Jesus—thank you for stopping my Tahoe that day in the fall of '09 and showing me tangibly the beauty of grace.

Notes

Introduction

1. Robert Frost, *Mountain Interval: The Road Not Taken* (New York: Henry Holt and Company, 1920), 9–10.
2. *Wikipedia*, s.v., "false peak," https://en.wikipedia.org/wiki/false_peak.

Chapter 1: The Way of Perfection

1. Winston Churchill, "Winston Churchill Quotes," AZ Quotes, 2014, http://www.azquotes.com/quote/394363.
2. David Benner, *The Gift of Being Yourself* (Downers Grove, IL: InterVarsity, 2004), 61.
3. Frost, *Mountain Interval*, 10.
4. Brené Brown, *Daring Greatly* (New York: Penguin Group, 2012), 69.
5. *Your Dictionary*, s.v. "legalism," http://www.yourdictionary.com/legalism.
6. Brown, *Daring Greatly*, 130.
7. Edward Welch, *When People Are Big and God Is Small* (Phillipsburg, NJ: P&R, 1997), 100.

Chapter 2 The Way of Secrets

1. L. Frank Baum, "The Royal Chariot Arrives," in *The Road to Oz*, 2004, http://www.pagebypagebooks.com/L_Frank_Baum/The_Road_to_Oz/The_Royal_Chariot_Arrives_p1.html.
2. Alan Turing, *The Imitation Game*, IMDb, 2014, http://www.imdb.com/title/tt2084970/quotes.
3. Frederick Buechner, "Telling Secrets Quotes," Good Reads, 2016, https://www.goodreads.com/work/quotes/118704-telling-secrets.
4. John Townsend, *Hiding from Love* (Grand Rapids: Zondervan, 1996), 158.
5. Buechner, "Telling Secrets Quotes."
6. Ibid.
7. Townsend, *Hiding from Love*, 162.

Chapter 3 The Way of the Monster

1. C. S. Lewis, *Surprised by Joy: The Shape of My Early Life* (New York: Harcourt Brace, 1955), 114.

2. Charles Dickens, *A Tale of Two Cities* (Mineola, NY: Dover Publications, 1999), 1.

3. Townsend, *Hiding from Love*, 93–94.

4. Dayna Drum, "It's Time to Address Spiritual Abuse in the Church," *Relevant*, October 27, 2014, http://www.relevantmagazine.com/god/church/its-time-address-spiritual-abuse-church.

Chapter 4 The Way of Medicating

1. J. K. Rowling, *Harry Potter and the Goblet of Fire* (New York: Arthur A. Levine Books, 2000), 695.

2. Cornell, *28 Days*, IMDb, 2000, http://www.imdb.com/title/tt0191754/quotes.

Chapter 5 The End of My Ways

1. Lynn Hirshberg, "The Misfit," *Vanity Fair* 54, no. 4 (April 1991), 160–69, 196–202.

2. Edward Welch, "Who Are We? Needs, Longings, and the Image of God in Man," *Premise* IV, no. 4 (December 1997), 8, http://pcahistory.org/HCLibrary/capo/premise/97/dec/p08.html.

3. John Baker, *Life's Healing Choices* (New York: Howard Books, 2007), 4.

4. John Piper, "Blessed Are the Poor in Spirit Who Mourn," Desiring God, February 2, 1986, http://www.desiringgod.org/messages/blessed-are-the-poor-in-spirit-who-mourn.

5. Benner, *Gift of Being Yourself*, 58.

Chapter 6 The Way of Hope

1. James Brown, "James Brown Quotes," Brainy Quotes, 2016, http://www.brainyquote.com/quotes/quotes/j/jamesbrown131783.html.

2. Charles Spurgeon, "Rest, Rest," no. 969, *The Spurgeon Archive*, January 8, 1871, http://www.spurgeon.org/sermons/0969.php.

3. Pauline Phillips, "Pauline Phillips Quotes," Brainy Quotes, 2016, http://www.brainyquote.com/quotes/keywords/sinners/html.

Chapter 7 The Way of Community

1. C. JoyBell C., "C. JoyBell C. Quotes," Good Reads, 2016, http://www.goodreads.com/quotes/894500-you-can-run-away-from-yourself-so-often-and-so.

2. Benner, *Gift of Being Yourself*, 52.

3. Robert D. Putnam, "About the Book," *Bowling Alone: The Collapse and Revival of American Community*, 2016, http://bowlingalone.com.

4. Peter Block, *Community: The Structure of Belonging* (Oakland, CA: Berrett-Koelher Publishers, 2008), 1–2, emphasis added.

5. Timothy Keller, *Counterfeit Gods* (New York: Riverhead Books, 2009), 20.

6. For a great book on this topic, see Eric Michael Bryant, *Not Like Me* (Grand Rapids: Zondervan, 2010).

7. John Ortberg, *The Me I Want to Be* (Grand Rapids: Zondervan, 2010), 182.

8. http://www.morphonline.org.

9. Larry Crabb, *Inside Out* (Colorado Springs: NavPress, 2013), 139.

10. See Ephesians 6:12.

11. Welch, "Who Are We?"

12. J. Keith Miller, *The Secret Life of the Soul* (Nashville: Broadman & Holman, 1997), 178.

Chapter 8 The Way of Work

1. Townsend, *Hiding from Love*, 96.

2. Henry Ford, "Henry Ford Quotes," Good Reads, 2016, https://www.goodreads.com/quotes/search?utf8=%E2%9C%93&q=henry+ford&commit=Search.

3. Donald Miller, *Scary Close* (Nashville: Nelson Books, 2014), xv.

4. Dictionary.com, s.v. "vulnerable," http://www.dictionary.com/browse/vulnerable.

Chapter 9 The Way of *More* Work

1. A. S. King, "Please Ignore Vera Dietes Quotes," Good Reads, 2016, http://www.goodreads.com/work/quotes/6860540-please-ignore-vera-dietz.

2. Beth Moore, "So Long Insecurity Quotes," Good Reads, 2016, http://www.goodreads.com/work/quotes/7026187-so-long-insecurity-you-ve-been-a-bad-friend-to-us.

3. Bisco Hatori, "Ouran High School Host Club, Vol. 7 Quotes," Good Reads, 2016, http://www.goodreads.com/work/quotes/473387-7.

4. Richard Rohr, "Grieving as Sacred Space," John Mark Ministries, January 3, 2003, http://www.jmm.org.au/articles/1266.htm.

5. Ortberg, *Me I Want to Be*, 16.

Chapter 10 The Way of Bravery

1. Madeleine L'Engle, "Madeleine L'Engle Quotes," Good Reads, 2016, https://www.goodreads.com/author/quotes/106.Madeleine_L_Engle.

2. Veronica Roth, "Allegiant Quotes," Good Reads, 2016, http://www.goodreads.com/work/quotes/15524549-allegiant.

3. Juliette Lewis, "Juliette Lewis Quotes," Good Reads, 2016, http://www.goodreads.com/author/show/7032007.Juliette_Lewis.

4. Brené Brown, "You Can Choose Courage or You Can Choose Comfort. You Cannot Choose Both," *Daring Greatly*, March 30, 2016, https://daringgreatly2016.wordpress.com/2016/03/30/you-can-choose-courage-or-you-can-choose-comfort-you-cannot-choose-both.

Melissa at Work

Melissa is currently on staff at Gateway Church in Austin, Texas. In addition, she is a highly engaging and well-respected inspirational speaker, a personal and spiritual development coach, a teacher, and an author.

Melissa's life experience has given her a depth of understanding tempered with compassion, love, and empathy. It has given her a story and God has given her a voice. She courageously lives her life as a missionary, allowing him to instruct, to guide, and to provide. She passionately, purposefully, and patiently follows him wherever he leads. And, wherever she goes, she beautifully reflects the heart of her Savior as she preaches good news to the poor, heals the brokenhearted, and announces his freedom to captives (Isa. 61:1).

Melissa at Play

Melissa is an avid hiker, a trail runner, a lover of the outdoors, a gardening and guitar-playing novice, and a paddleboarding enthusiast. Whenever possible, she and her two labs can be found soaking in God's beauty in the mountains and trails of Colorado.

Melissa Fisher is a faithful friend, a committed follower of Christ, and a treasure, who enriches the lives of many.

Hi. Melissa here.

I would love to hear from you. The best way to reach me depends on your inquiry.

You can follow me on **Twitter** @MelissaLFisher or like me on **Facebook** at The Way Of Hope group page. I also have an **Instagram** @GoTheWayOfHope and you can follow my **blog** or connect with me at **GoTheWayOfHope.com**.

In *The Way of Hope*, I share with you several things that have been integral in my healing journey. I also encourage you to check out the following sites:

- Gateway Church - GatewayChurch.com
- Destiny Project - DestinyProjectOnline.com
- Discovery Austin - DiscoveryPrograms.org
- The Ultimate Journey - UltimateJourney.org

Melissa Fisher

BakerBooks
a division of Baker Publishing Group
www.BakerBooks.com

Available wherever books and ebooks are sold.

LIKE THIS
BOOK?
Consider sharing
it with others!

- Share or mention the book on your social media platforms. Use the hashtag **#TheWayOfHope**.

- Write a book review on your blog or on a retailer site.

- Pick up a copy for friends, family, or strangers— anyone who you think would enjoy and be challenged by its message.

- Share this message on Twitter or Facebook: **"I loved #TheWayOfHope by @MelissaFisher // GoTheWayOfHope.com @ReadBakerBooks"**

- Recommend this book for your church, workplace, book club, or class.

- Follow Baker Books on social media and tell us what you like.

f Facebook.com/ReadBakerBooks

🐦 @ReadBakerBooks